# DESIGNING HOME INTERIORS

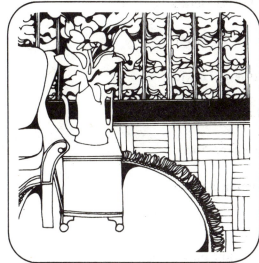
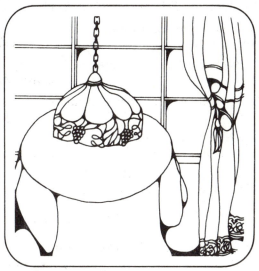

## A Study Guide

Winifred Yablonski
and Carolyn Breeden

Coast Community College District and
Rancho Santiago Community College District

# Credits

Chancellor, Coast Community College District  Norman E. Watson

President, Coastline Community College ............. Bernard J. Luskin

Executive Producer of Telecourses, KOCE-TV ........ Donald Gerdts

Director, Telecourse Design, Coastline
   Community College ........................................... Thomas H. Gripp

Telecourse Editor, Coastline Community
   College .................................................... Louise Matthews Hewitt

Superintendent, Rancho Santiago Community
   College District ..................................................... John E. Johnson

Assistant Superintendent, Rancho Santiago
   Community College District ................................. Richard Sneed

Dean of Instructional Services, Santa Ana
   Community College ................................................ Donna Farmer

DESIGNING HOME INTERIORS Course Team:

Instructional Designer, Coastline Community
   College ............................................................. Leslie Noble Purdy

Producer/Director, KOCE-TV .................................... Kent Johnson

Editor, Coastline Community College ...... Victoria Wind Hamilton

Illustrator .............................................................. Martha L. Lothers

Library of Congress Cataloging in Publication Data
Yablonski, Winifred, 1941-
    Designing home interiors.

    Includes bibliographical references.
    1. Interior decoration—Study and teaching.
I.  Breedon, Carolyn, 1944–      joint author.
II.  Coast Community College District. III. Rancho
Santiago Community College District. IV. Title.
NK2116.4.Y3        747'.8'83        78-18004
ISBN 0-8087-2509-2 pbk.

Library of Congress Number: 78-18004
International Standard Book Number: 0-8087-2509-2(paper)
Copyright © 1978 by Coastline Community College for Coast
Community College District and Rancho Santiago Community
College District.
J  I  H  G  F  E  D  C  B

# Contents

# Preface

We have written this book with a two-fold purpose: to share our enthusiasm for interior design, and to help you in the continuing process of discovering your talents. We hope that this guide will expand your awareness of the importance of interior design, and help you to create an interior environment that satisfies both you and your family.

We present guidelines, processes, and experiences that have been proven successful in developing an ability to plan and evaluate well-designed, functional interiors. You will discover that a well-planned home results when you know how to achieve a balance between those things that constitute good design and your personal expression.

The concepts presented here in the guide have worked well for professional interior designers and continue to work for us. We know they can work for you, too.

Winifred Yablonski
Instructor
Santa Ana
Community College

Carolyn Breeden
Instructor
Santa Ana
Community College

# Notes to the Student

The telecourse *Designing Home Interiors* promises to be an exciting learning experience for all of you who participate fully. But to glean as much enjoyment and information as possible from this course, you must approach it somewhat differently than you would a college-level, on-campus course. A television course or "telecourse" is a carefully structured learning system consisting of several interrelated parts. Each component—television programs, required textbook, this study guide, and the student packet—is very important in itself, but together they form a stronger whole.

This study guide will help you organize your approach to the course; it will introduce a wealth of design information, and will tell you, unit by unit, what you are expected to know at the completion of each lesson.

To complete this course successfully, you must watch all thirty of the television programs, read the assigned pages in your text, and complete each unit in this guide, as well as follow the instructions given in it. Please do not try to take notes during the television programs. Note-taking will only distract you. Watch the programs for important points and general content.

*Designing Home Interiors: A Study Guide* is divided into several parts.

- The "Assignments" tell you how to approach each unit. Follow the order that is indicated for each component of the lesson. For example, read the assigned segments of your study guide unit for each lesson first. Then watch the television program, and read the assigned pages in your text, *Beginnings of Interior Environment*, by Phyllis Allen, before going on to the remainder of your study guide.

- The "Overview" is partially a summary of the lesson's content. The overview highlights information found in both the television program and textbook, and, in addition, presents some facts found only in this guide.

- The "Student Learning Objectives" tell you what you are expected to know after completing each unit of study. These objectives will help you study for examinations. After you finish each lesson, review the objectives to determine if you can successfully meet them.

- The "Learning Supplement" adds important additional design information. Consumer tips are offered in this section.

- The "Key Terms and Concepts" are the major points and terms of the unit. Let this section act as a type of lesson outline for you as well as a vocabulary list.

- The "Learning Activities" offer you the chance to test what you have learned in each lesson. Answer the questions fairly; the key to successful self-testing is to recite the answers to questions without reference to a book or your notes. If you cannot complete each question, review the reading assignment and perhaps watch the television program again, if it is possible to do so. It is very important to realize that these questions and activities were designed to prepare you for examinations. In some of the units you will find assignments made in reference to your textbook (in addition to the reading assignment listed in the beginning of each study guide unit). For example, the Learning Activities may indicate that you "complete the assignment on page XXX of your text with these exceptions. . . ." Then you turn to page XXX in your text and find another set of assignments and instructions. **Follow the instructions and assignments as they are given in this study guide.** Even if the assigned readings in the textbook include an assignment or activity, complete them **only if it is assigned in this guide** (or as your local instructor indicates). Also found in the Learning Activities section are references to and assignments in the Student Packet.

■ The "Optional Activities" are given for those of you who wish to pursue a particular activity further than required in this course. Often you may want to complete the optional activities "just for fun."

■ The "Optional Readings" are found at the end of each unit in this study guide. They include sources of additional information for those interested in exploring a topic in detail or beyond the scope of this course.

*The Student Packet* is an assortment of activity cards packaged separately that allow you to practice what you have learned about floor plans, mixing colors, furniture arrangement, and the like. You may use crayons, colored pencils, colored markers, paints, or whatever you have available to complete your activity cards.


**Before You Begin**

Some students approach a telecourse with the notion that completing it will be a "snap." However, in this course, *Designing Home Interiors,* you will be learning a great deal about interior design at quite a fast pace. Therefore, complete your reading assignments, projects, or activities each week. It is all too easy to fall behind in your work. Use the Student Learning Objectives to tell you what to study, and use the Learning Activities to tell you how to study.

The overall goals of this telecourse are:

■ To provide students with fundamental skills necessary for planning home interiors that are functional, aesthetically attractive, and economically feasible.

- To provide consumer information essential to the selection of quality furnishings and materials appropriate for various design plans.

- To demonstrate ways that students can utilize existing furnishings and incorporate them into an overall plan.

- To identify methods used to create a home environment that express the personalities of people within.

- To identify interior design career opportunities and the educational background helpful to those planning to enter this profession.

Even though just one course will not make you a professional interior designer, we hope that you become excited about the field and continue to grow in your creative abilities.

# WHERE TO BEGIN

## 1

## BEGIN

The Emphasis Is on People

**Assignments for Unit One**

1. Read the Overview, Student Learning Objectives, and Learning Supplement for this unit.

2. Watch Television Program One, "Where to Begin."

3. Read pages xix-xxi in the Introduction, and pages 47-49 in Part 3 of *Beginnings of Interior Environment.*

4. Scan Part 1 and Part 2 of your text.

5. Consider Key Terms and Concepts.

6. Complete the Learning Activities.

7. Review the Student Learning Objectives.

## Overview

What does interior design mean to you? Interior design involves creating not only an aesthetically pleasing environment but also one that is functionally and psychologically acceptable. Well-designed interiors are based on the interrelationships of structure, furnishings, and environment, with the personalities and life styles of the people who live within. Interiors that are beautiful but fail to satisfy living needs are poorly designed. Equally dissatisfying are extremely functional interiors that project a cold, sterile, impersonal mood, as well as designs that are both functional and beautiful but inappropriate for the family. But it is possible to successfully combine both functional and aesthetic requirements in an interior by taking the time to develop a carefully thought out plan based on your specific needs. The basis of interior design is knowing how to use space and select and arrange furnishings to enrich various life styles.

Although there are several different factors to consider in planning, the greatest importance should be placed on individual and family life styles. This includes such things as the number and ages of people, resources, values, personalities, tastes, and interpersonal relationships. In other words, how does each person like to live and what are the living patterns of the family as a whole? If you do not have a thorough understanding of the life styles expressed within your family, it may be helpful to begin writing down your thoughts, reviewing, and revising them over a period of several days.

If the cost of implementing your design plan requires that the family give up a treasured weekend retreat, eating out, or other experiences of importance, it is essential to look at the plan again to determine if costs can be reduced or if "trade-offs" represent a satisfactory solution. If the home is truly in need of interior changes to improve the family's enjoyment and quality of life, perhaps it may warrant giving up, if only temporarily, a few other things of value. "Trade-offs" involve each person in the family, and, therefore, such decisions should include input from the individuals involved.

Your time and abilities are invaluable resources that need consideration during the financial planning stage of your design project. If you are going to tackle some of the work yourself, make sure you have the necessary knowledge and skills required to complete a quality job. But evaluate the amount of time required to complete the work with the amount of satisfaction gained. Sometimes it is wiser in the long run to pay someone else to do some of the work when you can, perhaps, derive more pleasure, save money, or spend your time more efficiently completing other tasks.

Oftentimes, the most difficult part of interior design can be knowing how or where to begin your project. Lack of information, too much information, too many ideas, or not knowing what to do first can lead to confusion from the start. This lesson suggests background steps considered essential to planning interiors. At this stage, you may not know how to totally evaluate, design, or develop a complete plan, but you can initiate several of the ideas that make interior design work for you. For example, with no knowledge about interior design, you can begin to develop a worthwhile resource file. Then as you work through each lesson, you will acquire the ability to complete the remaining steps in the overall plan.

Knowledge and application of basic terminology and design principles are essential to the development and evaluation of your plans. If you are an aware and informed consumer, you will find that this can help solve design problems and provide better, more effective communication with craftsmen, manufacturers, retailers, and others. As you learn to work with the principles of design, remember that they should serve as guidelines, not rules. If this is your first exposure to design, the easiest route to success is to apply them. However, as you acquire more experience, you will learn that, occasionally, some problems can be solved more creatively by working contrary to these principles.

To prevent wasting time searching through masses of magazines and clippings, create a system for organizing good design information and ideas that you collect. File these resources by types of rooms or by specific categories, such as good color schemes or storage ideas. Go through the file periodically, not only for ideas, but to eliminate those you no longer find appealing. This will help you begin to see a relationship among the remaining ideas that can further your understanding of your tastes in interior design. Identifying what you dislike is as important as knowing what you like in helping prevent confusion or errors in design decisions.

In addition to magazines and newspapers, take advantage of other resources for ideas—displays, friends' homes, and exhibitions. You can even increase your design knowledge while waiting in line or in an office. Look around you and analyze the area. Really learn to become more aware of the visual, functional, and psychological impact of your various surroundings.

When you have acquired a basic understanding of interior design guidelines and know the specific factors that should influence your selections, you are ready to develop a complete plan. If there is a cardinal rule in interior design (and this cannot be stressed enough) it is: *Always work with a complete, well thought-out plan.* Whether you are designing a simple storage unit or an entire home, have your ideas firmly in mind and on paper. This provides the opportunity to correct mistakes in the planning process rather than having to live with the frustration of mistakes.

Throughout this course, keep in mind that a satisfactory interior design plan incorporates function, economy, beauty, and individuality into a unique whole. But you can learn only so much from interior design books. The remainder rests with you. Continued self-education, practice, and experience make the written words come alive.

## Student Learning Objectives

When you complete Unit One, you should be able to do the following:

- Define interior design.
- Discuss the psychological and functional relationship of interior design to a satisfying home environment.
- Identify three primary factors that should be considered when establishing an interior plan. Discuss each factor as it relates to the overall plan.

## Learning Supplement

In the past, the term *interior decorating* was most frequently associated with "beautifying the home." Professionals responsible for this type of work were "interior decorators." Because we now use the terms *interior design* and *interior designer,* there seems to be some confusion about the differences.

Interior decorating projects usually include the adornment and embellishment of a home environment. Interior design, however, involves creating a total aesthetic environment. In addition, interior design places particular emphasis on satisfying the functional and psychological needs of the people within that environment. The main difference between design and decoration is that design involves devising a complete plan that interrelates the basic structure and the furnishings with the life styles, preferences, values and resources of the persons involved.

## Key Terms and Concepts

Interior design

Well-designed plan

Function

Economy

Beauty

Individuality

Life style

## Learning Activities

- Analyze the relationship of function, economy, beauty, and individuality to a well-designed interior plan.

- Using this guide, the program, and your own ideas, explain how a well-designed plan could improve the quality of your own interior environment for you and your family.

- Evaluate the importance of your time and abilities with reference to implementing interior design plans.

- List and consider at least five factors that would influence your interior design plans. Briefly explain the relationship of each factor to your design decisions.

- Devise an organized system for filing interior design ideas and articles you collect.

## Optional Activities

- Using your newspapers, advertising supplements, local magazines, and telephone directory, make a list of at least ten resources of design ideas available to you.

- Begin listing all activities and comments about how your family lives. Keep reviewing and adding to the list for several days. When the list appears complete, draw conclusions about the life styles expressed within your family, and how the interior environment should function to satisfy your needs.

## Optional Readings

*Better Homes and Gardens Decorating Book.* 3rd edition. Des Moines: Meredith Corporation, 1975. Pages 9–24. Well-written chapter on the importance of identifying life styles before beginning an interior plan.

Faulkner, Ray, and Faulkner, Sarah. *Inside Today's Home.* New York: Holt, Rinehart and Winston, 1975. Pages 3–29. Excellent information on factors to consider when planning a life space. Good discussion of the four major goals in planning home interiors.

Sulahria, Julie, and Diamond, Ruby. *Inside Design: Creating Your Environment.* San Francisco: Canfield Press, 1977. Pages 2–15. Good content on the relationship and importance of our interior space plans to our life styles.

# DOLLARS AND SENSE

## 2

Plan Ahead and Spend Wisely

**Assignments for Unit Two**

1. Read the Overview, Student Learning Objectives, and Learning Supplement for this unit.

2. Watch Television Program Two, "Dollars and Sense."

3. Read pages 315-16 and 331-33 in Part 11 of *Beginnings of Interior Environment.*

4. Review the Overview for this unit.

5. Consider Key Terms and Concepts.

6. Complete the Learning Activities.

7. Review the Student Learning Objectives.

**Overview**

Successfully designed interiors don't just happen! And no amount of luck or sheer magic will camouflage or compensate for the lack of good planning. Unit One, "Where to Begin," established that the development of a complete interior plan is one of the essential steps in making interior design work for you. Without one, failure is almost a guarantee. Although creating a plan cannot insure total success, it will certainly provide less chance for error and give you the opportunity to see a proposed end result before spending any money.

Initial planning can also help you evaluate your design choices in relation to your resources. For example, if the plan seems too costly to implement, you can identify possible ways to reduce expenditures. Or you may recognize that your original choices are going to require too much time or money to maintain them sufficiently. The important point is that you are able to evaluate a plan according to your needs, priorities, and resources before any commitment is made.

Although there is no rule that dictates the exact number or sequence of steps required for the development of a good interior plan, Program Two presents the primary factors that should be included and suggests one good sequence to follow. When you begin to apply these guidelines to your own situation you may think of one or two additional steps you would like to include, or perhaps you may choose a slightly different sequence. Note, however: it is important that you not omit any of the given factors and that you plan a logical, step-by-step sequence. For example, life styles must be identified before planning a furniture arrangement if a room is to function well and satisfy the needs of the individuals who use it.

Below is a review of the sequence of specific steps for interior plan development as presented in Television Program Two:

**Steps in Plan Development**

1. Identify life styles

2. Determine needs and wants in relation to life styles

3. Know your resources—human, financial, and material

4. Establish the theme or mood desired

5. Complete a floor plan evaluation

6. Complete a one-fourth-inch scale drawing of the floor plan

7. Arrange furniture templates and add built-in structures to the plan

8. Select samples for structural and portable furnishings

9. Visualize and evaluate the samples in relation to life styles, theme or mood desired, and design principles

10. Evaluate the total plan in relation to present resources

11. Revise the plan as needed

It is important to outline a sequential plan for the steps you will follow when designing your home, and the remaining lessons in this telecourse will help you to understand how to complete each step. Know what you need to complete and in what order, but at this time do not feel you should be prepared to execute each step. Future lessons include helpful information on such topics as furniture arrangement, fabric selection, and design principles.

Financial planning is another important consideration. One of the best ways to help you identify how much you might be able to spend on furnishings is to evaluate your income or the price of your dwelling in relation to percentages suggested by financial institutions. Remember these are only guidelines and should be analyzed with respect to your own situation and values.

The first expenditure plan, which includes projections for furnishings as well as major appliances, states that you should expect eventually to spend 25 to 33 percent of one year's gross income to complete an interior design plan. A second plan suggests that you estimate 25 to 33 percent of the dwelling's price as a base to be spent for furnishings. The figures obtained by these two methods may be vastly different, so be sure to evaluate them realistically. If you are furnishing a rental dwelling, use the annual-income formula.

After you know about how much you will spend for your furnishings, determine a period of time in which you feel you could reasonably handle the expenditures. It is not unusual to consider a three-to-five-year financial plan for completing the design of a larger dwelling. Also, if you prefer to spend a larger amount than suggested by the guidelines, you may find it necessary to divide the expenditures over a longer period.

When you do begin to purchase furnishings, think through the various ways you can pay for the products, and evaluate the methods to determine which ones suit you. In addition to paying cash, you may want to purchase some products on credit. The ninety-day plan is one form of credit purchasing that does not include a finance charge. Revolving charge accounts; loans from credit unions, banks, or financial companies; and credit extended by the retail stores involve interest charges that you should fully understand and calculate prior to signing the credit contract. It is possible and acceptable to shop for credit by comparing the annual percentage rates charged by the various companies. Because the annual rates can vary from approximately 9 percent to 30 percent, there can be a considerable dollar savings if you take the time to do some shopping for credit. Most consumers find that a combination of payment methods is most satisfactory.

Budgeting for furnishings is one of the most important aspects of successful interior designing. Few things can so quickly destroy your enthusiasm and your plans as overextending your budget. Therefore, recognize the importance of evaluating your design ideas in relation to your financial scheme and know how to make the best use of your money or credit when it is time to purchase the furnishings.

## Student Learning Objectives

When you complete Unit Two, you should be able to do the following:

- Explain the importance of developing a complete interior plan prior to making initial or additional purchases.

- Design a sequential pattern of essential steps for developing your interior plan.

- Identify and analyze, in relation to your life style, at least three guidelines that could be used when determining a design budget for your home.

## Learning Supplement

Because of the tremendous increase in the cost of homes during the past few years, it may be safer and more realistic to base your furnishings budget on income rather than price of the dwelling. However, it is suggested that you use both the price of the home and the annual-income guidelines to help you best evaluate how much to consider spending.

If you estimate your furnishings budget at 25 to 33 percent of one year's gross annual income, you may combine two incomes if there are two wage-earners in the home. However, it is a good idea to determine the following: Are the two wage-earners planning to continue working for a period of years? How stable or permanent are the present careers? Would there be a decrease in income if one were to change careers?

If you do plan to base a budget on a two-income figure, provide some kind of cushion to absorb the shock of emergencies or changes in plans. It would be wise to budget around the 25 percent guideline rather than the higher amount. Equally important: even if you plan to divide your expenditures over a period of several years, do not use projected cost-of-living or promotional raises in your planning.

## Key Terms and Concepts

Sequential interior-plan development

Furnishing-expenditure guidelines

Ninety-day plan

Credit

Annual percentage rate

Credit contract

**Learning Activities**

- Name two reasons for developing an interior-design plan before you purchase furnishings.

- Describe what is meant by sequential interior planning.

- List in sequence the essential steps for developing an interior plan. Explain why the order of this sequence is logical for the completion of the identified steps.

- Using the two guidelines presented in the program and study guide, identify how much a family with a $15,000 gross income could plan to spend for furnishing a $40,000 home.

- Discuss the primary disadvantage of paying cash for furnishings.

- Define the ninety-day payment plan. Explain the advantages of this method of payment.

- Describe how a knowledgeable consumer will shop for credit.

**Optional Readings**

*Better Homes and Gardens Decorating Book.* 3rd edition. Des Moines: Meredith Corporation, 1975. Pages 381–86. Good chart for determining cost of implementing design plans.

Stepat-DeVan, Dorothy. *Introduction to Home Furnishings.* New York: The Macmillan Company, 1971. Pages 247–55. Good explanation of finance charges, as well as ideas and suggestions for determining cost of implementing design plans.

Sulahria, Julie, and Diamond, Ruby. *Inside Design: Creating Your Environment.* San Francisco: Canfield Press, 1977. Pages 285–88, 300. Good consumer information on general budgeting and shopping for furniture.

# DESIGN

## BASICS

**3**

Understanding the Elements of Design

**Assignments for Unit Three**

1. Read the Overview, Student Learning Objectives, and Learning Supplement for this unit.

2. Watch Television Program Three, "Design Basics."

3. Read pages 63-83 in Part 4 of *Beginnings of Interior Environment*.

4. Consider Key Terms and Concepts.

5. Complete the Learning Activities.

6. Review the Student Learning Objectives.

## Overview

Design is everywhere around you. What you see, touch, and work with on a daily basis are examples of design and are composed of line, form or mass, space, color, and texture—the elements of design. Sometimes pattern and light are considered design elements as well. Pattern is made up of all the design elements, and light influences each element. Examine any object more closely. The lines of this object join together to create its form or mass. It is surrounded by space, defined as negative space, but it also occupies a specific area called positive space. Color and texture enhance its beauty and capture our attention.

One of your goals in interior design is to become consciously more aware of design. As your textbook states, the best way to learn to recognize the difference between good and bad design is to develop the habit of keen observation. You should learn to see how the various elements interrelate to produce a design. Really look at objects and become familiar with the use of line, form or mass, space, color, and texture. If you become perceptive and acquire the ability to observe, study, experiment, and analyze in this way, you will develop a sense of what constitutes good design.

Just as there is not a universal acceptance of one kind of beauty, neither are there any rigid rules that clearly delineate good design. Therefore, you should keep in mind that learning in the interior design field is not a matter of accepting standards set by others. It is a process of becoming more perceptive and developing your own ability to use the design elements. Rather than memorize rules, develop an appreciation of what factors have been proven successful in good design.

Everyone has his or her personal preferences, or what is sometimes called "personal taste." Even though we all feel that our personal taste is good taste, we still must be aware that our preferences may not always be an accurate assessment of good design. Try to recognize good design in rooms, furniture, and various objects, even if they do not express your own taste. Probably, in the process of developing an appreciation of good design, you will find that your own personal preferences change, evolve, and grow through this course of study. Keep in mind, not only that the elements of design are essential in any design, but also that knowing how to use them effectively is one of the best ways to personalize your own decorating schemes.

As you view the program, be aware of the methods and criteria used to analyze and evaluate home furnishings and room settings. Observe how the elements—line, form and mass, space, and texture—interrelate to create a total composition or complete design.

Note that the creative and effective use of the elements of design can make it possible to camouflage or correct undesirable effects in an overall design. Small areas can be made to appear larger, while vast areas can be made to feel more intimate. Once you have acquired an understanding of the design elements, you will find it easier to tailor visual space to your needs.

## Student Learning Objectives

When you complete Unit Three, you should be able to do the following:

- Explain the importance of the design elements (line, form or mass, space, texture, and color) as they relate to an interior plan.

- Given one picture of a room setting, identify the elements of design. Analyze the relationships of form or mass, space, line, and texture to the overall design.

- Define structural and decorative design.

- Describe at least three steps that could be helpful in learning to evaluate design.

- Discuss the problems of defining good taste.

## Learning Supplement

Both your text and the program for this unit discuss in detail, and supply excellent examples of, the two broad categories of design—structural and applied decorative design. Structural design has little if any applied ornament. The structure itself determines the form of the design, and enrichment comes from the materials used. Decorative design relies on applied line, texture, or color to enhance the basic structure. Any applied design should be in keeping with the shape and function of the structure. Within these two categories you will perceive much overlapping, and you may sometimes find it difficult to separate the two. Remember that structural or decorative design must be planned to accommodate or enhance the functional and decorative purposes of the object.

## Key Terms and Concepts

Structural design

Decorative design

Good taste

Line

Form or mass

Texture

Negative space

Positive space

## Learning Activities

- Select a picture of a furnished room that you feel represents good structural and decorative design. Evaluate and discuss the designs according to the composition of the elements and the criteria established in your text and the program.

- Give a definition of good taste.

- List the elements of design, and establish reasons for their importance in interior design.

## Optional Activities

- Evaluate several pieces of furniture in your own home according to criteria established for good design.

- Try to determine through use of magazine clippings, showroom settings, or other sources how your own personal taste is not always a reflection of good design.

## Optional Readings

Faulkner, Ray, and Faulkner, Sarah. *Inside Today's Home.* New York: Holt, Rinehart and Winston, 1975. Pages 159–76. Excellent discussion of design elements.

Sulahria, Julie, and Diamond, Ruby. *Inside Design: Creating Your Environment.* San Francisco: Canfield Press, 1977. Pages 18–22. Excellent discussion of elements of design. Good suggested activities at the end of the section.

# PRINCIPLES OF DESIGN

**4**

Good Design Based on Principles

**Assignments for Unit Four**

1. Read the overview and Student Learning Objectives for this unit.

2. Watch Television Program Four, "Principles of Design."

3. Review pages 63–75 in Part 4 of *Beginnings of Interior Environment.*

4. Consider Key Terms and Concepts.

5. Complete the Learning Activities.

6. Review the Student Learning Objectives.

## Overview

Interior design should be based on the selection and arrangement of the design elements (line, form or mass, space, color, and texture) according to the principles of design. The principles of design—proportion, scale, balance, rhythm, emphasis, and harmony—are used to create an orderly and pleasing interior arrangement. To be able to differentiate between good and poor design, you must know and understand these six principles.

From the earliest times, men and women have tried to make their environments more pleasing. Gradually guidelines and principles were developed through observation of what is in nature and through studying those factors that brought acclaim to great works of art.

Proportion is interrelation of magnitude, quantity, and degree. Proportion is defined as the relation of one part to another or to the whole, or of one object to another. Although no foolproof system of proportioning has been devised that holds true in every situation, the "golden section," as discussed in your text, is widely accepted. Keep in mind that implementation of the "perfect proportions" established by the golden section can be limited by use, individual preferences, and materials.

Scale refers primarily to the size of objects in relation to other objects and to people. Scale is usually referred to as either large or small, depending on the point of comparison. Good scale is the result of a pleasing relationship of all components in a space. When selecting and organizing furnishings for an interior space, make sure that they are scaled to people, to each other, and to the space in which they will be used.

Balance in interior design is equilibrium as the eye perceives it. You will need to become familiar with the psychological effect of "visual balance" because objects tend to appear equalized in a space. When a room is well balanced, things look as if they belong where they are; it is a comfortable setting. Balance can be divided into three types: formal, informal, and radial. In formal balance, one side of an arrangement is the mirror image of the other. Equilibrium is easily achieved through the application of formal balance, as you will observe in many traditionally planned interiors. Informal balance is, perhaps, more difficult to achieve because there is no set formula for creating it. However, with a little imagination and creative arrangement, you can make the components of a design appear to have equal weight even though they are different. Radial balance results when there is circular movement from or toward a central point.

Rhythm is the intangible element of composition that keeps the eye traveling easily from one part of an arrangement to another. It contributes to the beauty of our interior living spaces by enhancing individuality and character. Rhythm makes our designs come alive through implied movement and direction. Refer to your text for a survey of ways rhythm may be achieved in your interior design.

The terms *dominance* and *subordination* are used to discuss emphasis. Dominance calls attention to more important parts of a composition; subordination can be thought of as a reduction of the competition in less important parts. Emphasis relieves monotony and helps create visual stimulation. When creating a pattern of emphasis, you should decide how important each unit should be, and then give it the proper amount of visual importance.

Harmony is achieved when all of the other five design principles are applied. Unit Five treats this subject extensively.

## Student Learning Objectives

When you complete Unit Four, you should be able to do the following:

- Define the following principles of design: proportion, scale, balance, rhythm, emphasis, and harmony.

- Given two pictures of chairs, select a correctly scaled table and lamp for each.

- Given linear wall space, select a correctly proportioned sofa length for that space.

- Explain the visual difference between formal and informal balance.

- Discuss the importance of allowing various segments within a room to carry differing amounts of emphasis.

- Identify three possible ways to achieve a major point of emphasis within a room.

- Evaluate one picture of a room setting according to the following principles of design: proportion and scale, balance, rhythm, and emphasis.

## Key Terms and Concepts

Balance

Proportion

Scale

Rhythm

Emphasis

"Golden section"

Subordination

Dominance

22

## Learning Activities

- Using either formal or informal balance, plan one functional furniture arrangement for a given area.

- Using graph paper, make a simple wall drawing that includes two chairs, a table with a lamp, and pictures behind the chairs. Make the furnishings fit proportions of a wall space that is nine feet wide by eight feet high. Using the "golden mean" found in your text, calculate the proportions and then arrange the furniture accordingly. Refer to page 69 of your text when necessary.

## Optional Activity

- Evaluate one of your own rooms according to the principles of design. Identify possible changes that would improve the room's design.

## Optional Readings

Alexander, Mary Jean. *Designing Interior Environment.* New York: Harcourt Brace Jovanovich, Inc., 1972. Pages 44–55. An introduction to design principles. Illustrations pertain to interiors.

Evans, Helen Marie. *Man the Designer.* New York: The Macmillan Co., 1973. Pages 52–66. Excellent discussion of the principles of design. Quality and varied illustrations. The author includes a section on the design principles in other cultures.

# THEMES

## AND MOODS

### 5

Harmony in Design

**Assignments for Unit Five**

1. Read the Overview and Student Learning Objectives for this unit.

2. Watch Television Program Five, "Themes and Moods."

3. Review pages 63-85 in Part 4 of *Beginnings of Interior Environment.*

4. Consider Key Terms and Concepts.

5. Complete the Learning Activities.

6. Review the Student Learning Objectives.

**Overview**

Have you ever walked into a room and felt that all its components work together? This unified feeling doesn't just happen. It results only when the room's entire design expresses all the principles of design.

Lesson Four, "Principles of Design," concentrated on five of the basic principles of design: proportion, scale, balance, rhythm, and emphasis. When these five have been successfully interrelated in one design, the last design principle, harmony, is usually achieved.

Harmonious rooms are based on a single theme or mood, such as informal or natural. Rooms that have this harmonious relationship may not reflect your personal taste, but you will generally find that the overall design is interesting and pleasing. The next time you view a room setting that you find attractive, try to determine why you feel the room is well designed. Most often, your eye will focus first on the major point of emphasis in the room and rhythmically travel to the other, less dominant, segments. The room will appear visually balanced, and all components will be in proportion to one another and to the room as a whole. The room and all its furnishings express a unified, harmonious theme because of the use and application of the design elements and principles.

To prevent monotony, a design plan must exhibit sufficient variety. For example, a room that has only one specific fabric texture would be plain and uninteresting because it would lack the balance of unity with variety. Therefore, try to "fine-tune" your senses so that you will recognize when a room has sufficient unity to be harmonious but also includes the variety necessary for interest.

One of the easiest ways to begin planning the design for a room is to select a theme or mood that will be compatible with your life style. Many different names can be used to identify possible themes, but it is usually easier to describe it according to its degree of formality. There is no specific number of degrees; rather, there is a range of possibilities between the most elegantly formal and the least formal, most rustic mood. In the television program for this unit you will see five different moods, each expressing a different degree of formality. A specific theme can be used throughout an entire home, or the moods can vary from room to room. However, when varying the themes, harmony throughout the home must be achieved through the use of an underlying, unifying factor such as color.

**Student Learning Objectives**

When you complete Unit Five, you should be able to do the following:

■ Discuss how harmony encompasses all other principles and elements of design, resulting in a single and orderly whole.

- List the six principles of design and explain the relationship of each to a good interior plan.

- Analyze two room settings according to the elements and principles of design used, and list changes that would improve the total design.

- Identify two different themes for a specified room and explain how to apply the elements and principles of design to achieve each theme.

**Key Terms and Concepts**

Theme (mood)

Harmony

Unity with variety

Principles of design

Degree of formality

**Learning Activities**

- Complete the assignment on pages 84-85 of your text.

- Define harmony.

- Explain what is meant by "unity with variety." Discuss its relationship to a well-designed room.

- Select a patterned fabric or wallpaper and explain how the principles of design have or have not been applied.

- Discuss the importance of establishing a room theme in the development of a unified plan for that room.

- Identify a theme for one room and select or describe a fabric, a floor covering, a wall covering, and one accessory expressing that theme.

**Optional Activities**

- Analyze a furnished room in a model home or in a retail store according to the principles of design. Identify possible changes that could improve the designs.

- Study the individual rooms in your home, and determine if each expresses a single theme.

**Optional Readings**

Alexander, Mary Jean. *Decorating Made Simple.* New York: Doubleday and Co., Inc., 1964. Pages 5–7. Discussion of how harmony or unity is achieved.

Faulkner, Ray, and Faulkner, Sarah. *Inside Today's Home.* New York: Holt, Rinehart and Winston, 1975. Page 186. Comprehensive discussion of harmony, variety, and unity.

Sulahria, Julie, and Diamond, Ruby. *Inside Design: Creating Your Environment.* San Francisco: Canfield Press, 1977. Pages 43–44. Defines harmony in relation to the elements and principles of design. Good suggested activities at the end of the section.

# MAPPING IT OUT

**6**

## How to Draw a Floor Plan

**Assignments for Unit Six**

1. Read the Overview and Student Learning Objectives for this unit.

2. Watch Television Program Six, "Mapping It Out," and refer to Figure 6.1 in this guide when necessary.

3. Study the floor plans and architectural symbols on pages 53–58 in your text, *Beginnings of Interior Environment*.

4. Consider Key Terms and Concepts.

5. Complete the Learning Activities.

6. Review the Student Learning Objectives.

## Overview

To furnish a room as quickly as possible, you may be tempted to skip some important preliminary design work. But avoid the temptation. It is extremely difficult, if not impossible, to develop a functional and attractive room if you do not follow the required steps for complete planning.

Unit One, "Where to Begin," stated the importance of complete plan development in successful interior design. As you begin the actual design process for your home, your first step should be to complete a one-fourth-inch scale drawing of the floor plan for each room you plan to furnish. These drawings should include all major architectural elements, such as fireplaces, doors, and built-ins, as well as the important electrical details, outlets, and architectural lighting.

Once you have completed the scale drawing for each room, you will be able to use furniture templates, or small patterns of the furniture pieces, to try out your ideas for furniture arrangements and additional built-ins before you actually begin purchasing. (Several sets of templates can be found in the Student Packet. Also, standard templates are available at stationery or artist supplies stores.) Templates will be more accurate than either a tape measure or guesswork in giving you a picture of how various pieces will work in the room. The entire family can participate in these planning stages before the final decisions are made. Quite often, older children truly enjoy developing plans for their own rooms.

There are so many benefits from planning on paper. Also, completed plans are helpful shopping tools. When you have a plan on paper to serve as a reminder of the exact sizes and pieces of furniture needed, you are able to avoid mistakes caused by impulse buying. If you expect to employ craftsmen to complete some of the interior work, these plans can help the workers have a more accurate understanding of exactly what your needs are. In addition, planning on paper provides an excellent opportunity to double-check your design ideas against the functional needs determined for the room. Traffic patterns can be evaluated and any deficiencies corrected before you begin the implementation of the plan.

When you view the television program, pay close attention to the equipment suggested for completing scale drawings. Although not all pieces are absolutely essential, those shown will help you complete the work as quickly and accurately as possible. For example, you may draw your plan on plain paper, but scale conversion is easier when using one-fourth-inch grid graph paper. (Note that this can be found in the Student Packet.)

Be sure to make an initial sketch of the entire room. Although the sketch is not drawn to scale, record all the essential measurements accurately on the sketch. Identify the exact location of all architectural and electrical details that should be included on your plans.

The program points out how you can apply the same techniques when making elevation drawings of specific walls. Although scaled elevation drawings are not necessary at this time, knowing how to use this information will be helpful in future lessons. Pages 259 and 282-83 in your text provide good examples of wall elevations with and without the inclusion of furniture. Note that the elevations in the text are shown as extensions of the floor plan rather than being illustrated separately, as shown in the television program.

### Student Learning Objectives

When you complete Unit Six, you should be able to do the following:

■ Given a scale floor plan and wall elevations for one room, identify and accurately describe in detail all architectural and electrical symbols used in the plan.

■ Using a one-fourth-inch scale, accurately reproduce a floor plan of a given room.

■ Explain the value of completing one-fourth-inch-scale drawings of rooms to be furnished.

### Key Terms and Concepts

One-fourth-inch scale

Architectural scale

Architectural symbols

Electrical symbols

Elevation drawings

Templates

### Learning Activities

■ Draw the following architectural and electrical symbols: telephone jack, recessed light fixture, switch, duplex outlet, and half-hot outlet.

■ Give two good reasons for completing a scale floor-plan drawing of a room you plan to furnish.

■ Using the following measurements, draw lines indicating their conversion to one-fourth-inch scale: 6'2", 2'6", 15', and 7'10".

■ Accurately reproduce to one-fourth-inch scale a floor plan for one room you will be furnishing. Include all essential architectural and electrical symbols.

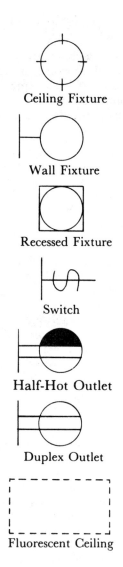

Figure 6.1 Electrical Symbols

## Optional Activities

- Using the floor plan drawn for the last Learning Activity in this unit, complete a one-fourth-inch scale elevation drawing of one wall that has at least one architectural detail, such as a fireplace, door, window, or built-in unit.

- Select an architectural blueprint of the floor plan for a home, and identify as many of the components as possible.

## Optional Reading

Sherwood, Ruth F. *Homes—Today and Tomorrow.* Peoria, Illinois: Charles A. Bennett Company, Inc., 1972. Pages 119–21. Good explanation of how to read a blueprint.

# TAKE THE FIRST STEP

## 7

The Key Is a Good Plan

**Assignments for Unit Seven**

1. Read the Overview, Student Learning Objectives, and Learning Supplement for this unit.

2. Watch Television Program Seven, "Take the First Step," and refer to Figure 7.1 when necessary.

3. Read pages 47-58 in Part 3 of *Beginnings of Interior Environment.*

4. Consider Key Terms and Concepts.

5. Complete the Learning Activities.

6. Review the Student Learning Objectives.

**Overview**

Planning for interior design all too often comes as an afterthought when it is, in fact, of primary concern. A thorough, careful evaluation of the basic floor plan and structural details of a home paves the way to a complete interior plan and should be considered before any final decision in home buying or remodeling is made.

Many problems that commonly arise during the interior design process could easily be minimized, or even eliminated, if such an evaluation were made early. Even though a poorly designed dwelling can sometimes be "salvaged" by a successful interior-furnishings plan, developing a beautiful, functional home is easier and more economical if you begin with a good floor plan. But remember that what constitutes an "ideal plan" is determined by individual life styles, preferences, and resources.

Certainly very few people today enjoy the luxury of a custom-built home. Therefore, it may be close to impossible to find a pre-built home that meets your every requirement, but it is possible to find one that satisfies most of them. With this attitude in mind, one can consider workable "trade-offs" and still find a very suitable dwelling. Because no two individuals or families have the same needs, it is impossible to describe a perfect living space. However, there are several ways to scrutinize plans.

Basically, floor plans can be classified as closed, open, or combination plans. Closed plans are based on traditional concepts of separate rooms for separate activities. This type of planning allows for maximum privacy, variation in simultaneous activities, temperature control in specific areas, and traffic flow to each room without crossing through another. If closed plans are furnished traditionally, they may require specific pieces of furniture. Therefore, it may be difficult to have the room function in a variety of ways. Construction costs are generally higher in this type of plan also.

The open plan calls for enclosed spaces for bedrooms and bathrooms with only partial or no specific divisions for the remaining activity and support areas. The most important advantages of open plans are as follows: They are less costly to construct; they appear larger than a closed-plan interior with the same space; they provide occasion for more interaction among family members in spaces that can be used for multiple activities. Conversely, open plans may afford neither the necessary individual privacy nor the desired noise and temperature control. In addition, if multipurpose rooms are to be utilized as fully as planned, furniture selection and arrangement is crucial.

Many dwellings constructed today reflect a combination of both types of plans. The combination plan incorporates private bedroom and bath spaces, specific rooms for specific activities (such as living rooms and dining rooms) with multipurpose areas (kitchen/family rooms or general activity rooms).

Another way of analyzing a floor plan is in reference to the use of space defined as group space, private space, and support space. Group spaces, those areas set aside for living, recreation, hobbies, and eating, are generally planned to accommodate two or more people and to provide for interaction among family members and friends. However, we are becoming increasingly aware of the need for each person to have what is known as "private space"—a room, or at least a portion of a room, set aside for individual, quiet pursuits, or simply a place to escape the stresses of the outside world. Although bedrooms and bathrooms are usually designated as private space areas, in smaller homes or homes with larger families it may be necessary to consider private space provisions in other rooms.

In addition, there are further basic requirements common to all well-designed residential plans, and any dwelling may be evaluated with reference to these. Your text provides guidelines to use when further assessing a floor plan.

Facilities and systems providing for heating and cooling, electricity, plumbing, laundry, and storage should be adequate for the home and its occupants and should be easily accessible. Lack of storage areas represents one of the major deficiencies in contemporary homes. Therefore, built-in storage should be scrutinized for quality of materials, construction details, and its adaptability to specific needs.

Keep in mind the possibility of using some rooms in ways other than those intended by the builder. For example, a dining room can become a music room or a hobby room. Likewise, you may need to analyze the opportunities for creating multipurpose areas within single rooms. To evaluate a plan realistically and successfully, you must identify how it presently meets your needs, and how in the future you might increase the functional qualities of the home without exceeding your budget.

Other considerations could include the number and placement of electrical outlets, structural lighting, type and use of various building materials, the inclusion of fire-detection systems, burglary prevention devices, and extended spaces. The garage and outdoor living areas—extended spaces—can increase the serviceability of your home if they are planned so as to meet the deficiencies of the interior plan.

With pencil and paper in hand, list the positive and negative aspects of each specific area or room. Follow this with a summary of the plan as a whole. Knowing the positive features to be enhanced and the negative qualities to be overcome provides a foundation upon which to build the design of the interior. If the dwelling is furnished, look beyond the furnishings and determine whether your basic requirements are met.

When selecting housing of any type, remember that you should appraise the use and arrangement of available space, architectural details, and the type and quality of various fixtures and equipment—always with reference to your budget and individual needs.

**Student Learning Objectives**

When you complete Unit Seven, you should be able to do the following:

- Identify one advantage and one disadvantage of both closed-plan and open-plan interiors.

- List at least fifteen criteria established as essential to a well-designed residential floor plan.

- Using established criteria for a well-designed residential plan, analyze a specified floor plan.

- Evaluate a chosen floor plan in relation to a given family's life style, priorities, and resources.

**Learning Supplement**

Most people who spend considerable time, effort, and dollars creating an interior environment give little or no thought to securing their investments. Whether you rent or own your own home, one of the most important initial design steps should be to provide for the security and safety of the family as well as the furnishings.

At your request, most police departments will provide free burglary-prevention security checks for the home. This service usually includes an inspection of both the interior and the exterior of the residence. In addition to mentioning improvements such as locking mechanisms for doors, windows, gates, and fences, the officers may be prepared to suggest minor changes in exterior lighting and landscaping that would improve your security.

The local fire department also may offer free home-safety checks. Usually they propose installation of fire-prevention systems and smoke detectors and suggest escape routes to use in case of fire.

When selecting a home, you should consider external factors that influence the livability of that dwelling.

Although it is not complete, here is a list of some suggested external factors worth consideration.

- Sun exposure

- Location within development

- Privacy

- Size of yard
- Landscaping requirements
- Neighborhood
- Proximity of churches, schools, shopping centers, and recreational facilities
- Distance to place of employment
- Access to public transportation, airports, and highways
- Local insurance and tax rates
- Code restrictions

**Key Terms and Concepts**

Open plan

Closed plan

Combination plan

Well-designed plan

"Ideal plan"

Group, private, and support spaces

Extended spaces

"Trade-off"

Traffic patterns

**Learning Activities**

- Using the information found in this guide, your text, and the television program, evaluate any home other than your own as to its ability to satisfy the essential requirements of a good floor plan.

- Analyze your present living environment, keeping in mind your life style. Identify functional and aesthetic changes that could better satisfy your needs and priorities. What other changes might be necessary to accommodate a different life style sharing this same environment?

- Recall the couple that you viewed in Television Program Seven. Try to identify the important details observed by the couple and those they overlooked. How would you approach the same situation? What parts of the plan appeal to you? Why? What changes in this floor plan would improve its design? (Refer to Figure 7.1)

**Optional Activities**

- Contact your local law-enforcement agency and fire department to determine if free home-security and safety checks are

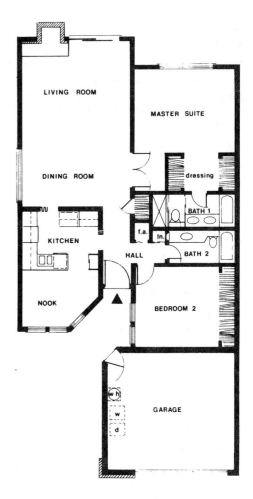

Figure 7.1

Floor Plan Evaluation

Reference. The plan evaluated in Program 7 is diagrammed here. Courtesy of Warmington Development, Inc., Shady Hollow Patio Homes.

available. Consider the advantages of these services in improving the protection of your home.

■ Select a different home in another location within your community. Examine its external factors and evaluate them with regard to your own priorities.

■ List your priorities regarding the external and internal features of a home. Be able to explain your choice.

## Optional Readings

Faulkner, Ray, and Faulkner, Sarah. *Inside Today's Home.* New York: Holt, Rinehart and Winston, 1975. Pages 3-136. Excellent discussion of interior space usage as well as open, closed, and combination plans.

Sulahria, Julie, and Diamond, Ruby. *Inside Design: Creating Your Environment.* San Francisco: Canfield Press, 1977. Pages 2–17 and pages 64–68. Outstanding in-depth discussion of the planning and evaluation of the various space divisions and systems within a home.

# FOCUS ON COLOR

**8**

Know the Terms and Elements

**Assignments for Unit Eight**

1. Read the Overview, Student Learning Objectives, and Learning Supplement for this unit.

2. Watch Television Program Eight, "Focus on Color." *Because the subject matter of this program and the next two is color, it is important that you view these television lessons on a well-tuned color television set.*

3. Read pages 89-118 in Part 5 of *Beginnings of Interior Environment.* Pay close attention to pages 93-113.

4. Consider Key Terms and Concepts.

5. Complete the Learning Activities.

6. Review the Student Learning Objectives.

## Overview

Color is usually considered the most dynamic and important element in interior design. Although not everyone perceives color in the same way, each person is affected by his/her own physical and psychological interpretations of the colors in his/her surroundings. It is virtually impossible to ignore or escape the impact of color. Therefore it is essential to develop a thorough understanding of color dimensions—hue, value, and intensity—so that you can create color plans that elicit the visual and psychological responses desired by each individual within your home.

Learning everything there is to know about color at one time can appear to be an overwhelming task. But if you learn the vocabulary of color and the general guidelines for its use in an interior, additional color information will be easier to understand and to incorporate into your knowledge.

The two color systems most commonly used in interior design are the Brewster System, which is based on pigments, and the Munsell System, which is based on light. While the Brewster System (used in Television Program Eight as the standard color wheel) is helpful in gaining an understanding of the basic hues and their relationships, the Munsell System is more beneficial when analyzing variations in the value and intensity (chroma) of the specific hues. The Munsell System is shown as the triangular color globe in Program Eight.

When you view Television Program Eight (be sure to watch it on a color television set) and read your text assignment, pay particular attention to the color vocabulary. Become familiar with words such as *value, neutralized, complementary,* and *analogous.* An ability to understand, correctly apply, and effectively communicate with this vocabulary is essential in the development of a working knowledge of color.

Although it is quite possible to plan well-designed rooms in opposition to the color application guidelines, generally it is easier for beginners to create rewarding color plans by adhering to the specific hue, value, and intensity distribution guidelines presented in the program and your text. Once you have developed confidence in working with these guidelines, experiment by varying or even ignoring the suggestions. For example, try using the most intense color on a large upholstered piece of furniture. Sometimes, breaking a rule can be very effective aesthetically. However, to avoid expensive mistakes, experiment in the planning stage. Mentally visualize the room and evaluate the effects prior to actually implementing your plan. Always use color samples—the larger, the better. To fully understand the application of this information, you must practice and experiment with colors and evaluate the results.

**Student Learning Objectives**

When you complete Unit Eight, you should be able to do the following:

- Identify the three basic divisions of hues on a color wheel that has twelve colors, and explain the components of each division.

- Define the following color dimensions: hue, value, intensity.

- Given five examples of room color plans, identify monochromatic, accented neutral, analogous, complementary, and triad color schemes.

- Identify the Munsell and Brewster color systems.

- Discuss the importance of considering the type and the amount of light when planning color for interiors.

- Given samples, select the best value and intensity of a color to create the specified visual illusions for each of five identified room problems.

- Define the "Law of Chromatic Distribution," and explain how this rule should be applied when planning color placement throughout a room.

**Learning Supplement**

One of the easiest ways to begin practicing and improving your understanding of the color dimensions and the application guidelines is to analyze the use of color in your immediate surroundings. For example, determine which values and intensities of specific hues create the coloring in a particular flower. What house colors appear to advance or stand out as compared to other house colors nearby?

Take advantage of all the numerous opportunities to refine your color skills. When you have free time, try using paint chips to develop attractive related and contrasting color schemes. Also, select a patterned fabric and use its colors to mentally plan a color scheme for an entire room. Try to visualize how the room would look and determine what changes would improve the plan. If you become more aware of all the color around, you will learn to work mentally with color and will refine your color skills.

**Key Terms and Concepts**

Hue

Value

Intensity

Primary

Secondary

Tertiary

Brewster System

Munsell System

Intensity distribution

Value distribution

Monochromatic

Accented neutral

Analogous

Complementary

Triad

Shade

Tone

Tint

**Learning Activities**

- Complete Color Cards One, Two, Three, and Four in the Student Packet. Follow the directions listed on pages 119-21 of your text.

- Using a color picture of a room, identify the specific hues found within the room. Determine where tints and shades of those hues have been used.

- Explain the guidelines for the distribution of color intensities within one room.

- Using any subject matter, identify a monochromatic, an analogous, and a complementary color scheme.

- Describe two ways one color can be used to help increase the apparent intensity of another color.

- Discuss the value of the Munsell Color System in interior design.

- Name the three secondary colors in the Brewster Color System.

- Describe one way color can be used to help solve each of the following room problems:

  a. The ceiling is too high.
  b. The room is too small.
  c. The room has structural component in an undesirable color.
  d. The room is very long and narrow.

- Define the following color terms: *hue, shade, tone, tertiary,* and *intensity.*

- Explain the importance of evaluating color samples in the location in which they will be used.

## Optional Activities

- Develop a complete color plan for one room. Analyze the effects on the plan when it is viewed in fluorescent light, incandescent light, and natural daylight.

- Select three patterned fabrics. View the fabrics at close range, and then at a distance. Explain any resulting changes in your perception.

- For a specified room create two individual color plans based on the colors found in the following: (1) a nature subject (such as a leaf or sunset) and (2) a painting or an art object.

## Optional Readings

Faulkner, Ray, and Faulkner, Sarah. *Inside Today's Home.* New York: Holt, Rinehart and Winston, 1975. Pages 191-210. Excellent coverage of color's three dimensions and use of color to solve design problems.

Itten, Johannes. *The Elements of Color.* New York: Van Nostrand Reinhold Company, 1970. Small book but excellent information on learning to work with the color dimensions. Theoretical but easy to read.

Sulahria, Julie, and Diamond, Ruby. *Inside Design.* San Francisco: Canfield Press, 1977. Pages 48-63. Excellent coverage of subject. Particularly easy to understand.

Whiton, Sherrill. *Interior Design and Decoration.* Philadelphia: J. B. Lippincott Company, 1974. Pages 438–53. Good in-depth explanation of the relationship between light and color. Good coverage of basic content of this lesson.

# COLOR

## 9

# INTERACTIONS

The Psychology of Color

**Assignments for Unit Nine**

1. Read the Overview and Student Learning Objectives for this unit.

2. Watch Television Program Nine, "Color Interactions." *Be sure to watch this program on a color television set.*

3. Review pages 89-93 in Part 5 of *Beginnings of Interior Environment.*

4. Consider Key Terms and Concepts.

5. Complete the Learning Activities.

6. Review the Student Learning Objectives.

## Overview

Are you aware that color has a psychological effect on you? Unfortunately, this fact is often overlooked by individuals when they are developing a color plan for their home. People of all ages express likes and dislikes for certain colors—and generally base their furnishing selections on these preferences. However, these opinions are expressed with little or no conscious realization of the impact that the color choices will have on emotions.

Color's three dimensions—hue, value, and intensity—and their effective use are some of the most helpful tools for achieving a desired mood within a room. For example, lower intensities and darker values such as brown and burgundy can create a warm, restful atmosphere. More intense, lighter-value colors such as sunny yellow and brilliant orange command more attention and produce a stimulating environment.

As you work toward developing the desired feeling for a room through a color plan, it is essential to recognize the effect that your color choices will have on the mood, behavior, and temperament of each family member. Although color research projects have provided many interesting findings related to human psychological and emotional reactions to color, there is no specific set of responses that pertains to every person. Also, it appears that our emotional reactions to color may be both inherent and learned through everyday experiences. Thus, it is possible for two people in the same family to react very differently to the same color. For example, one person may be happiest surrounded by a bright, crisp combination of red, yellow, and blue. But the other individual might either dislike living with one or more of these colors or find the grouping so stimulating that it becomes offensive.

Because any given color can evoke such a variety of psychological reactions, each family member should have the opportunity to respond to color schemes before final decisions are made. You may find that some changes in the original design are needed, but with thoughtful planning, it is possible to create a color scheme that will be satisfactory to all family members.

In addition to identifying personal responses, it is helpful to understand some of the more common general reactions to colors. Your text includes a chart of common reactions to warm and cool hues. Consider, too, the effects of varying the values and intensities of these specific hues.

Lesson Eight, "Focus on Color," explains how variations in color dimensions can produce illusory changes in a room setting and, in turn, how these visual effects can influence a person in that room. Walls treated with a light value of a cool color will tend to visually enlarge a room, which makes this type of treatment ideal for a person who requires a feeling of open space. But this would not be a wise wall-treatment choice for one who prefers a "closed-in," more protected, environment.

Additional factors that can influence psychological responses include the interrelationship of the color dimensions to one another, the functions of the room, the geographical area of your home, and the life style of the family members.

Generally plans that have greater contrasts between color dimensions induce higher levels of emotional excitement than do those having fewer contrasts. A plan that uses complementary colors and opposites in value and intensity ranges is an example. Likewise, plans incorporating several hues are more stimulating than those designed with no more than one or two. When the functions of a room include considerable physical activity, you may want to use color plans that elicit a similar emotional response. But this same color scheme would be inappropriate for a room planned for studying, reading, or resting.

Color and your home's geographic location are related, too. Because the type and amount of light in any room and the climatic conditions outside are determined by the location of your home, the colors to be chosen should compensate for the undesirable effects of geographic conditions. Color studies have proven that people feel physically warmer when surrounded by the warmer colors. Therefore, a home in a cold climate, when designed with warm colors, may be physically and psychologically more comfortable than one planned with cool colors. Rooms that receive very little light can appear somber and depressing, but warm colors in light values can give such rooms the illusion of an increased amount of sunlight and can diminish the effects of the exterior environment.

The life style of family members determines the functions of specific rooms and should influence the color choices you make. But even though life style may indicate one type of color choice, personal preference may dictate another. For example, you may prefer living with light values and want to have white carpeting, but such a decor would be a continuous source of frustration and dissatisfaction if you lack the time or the desire to provide the required maintenance.

**Student Learning Objectives**

When you complete Unit Nine, you should be able to do the following:

- Explain the impact of color's three dimensions—hue, value, and intensity—on psychological reactions. Describe the most common psychological reactions related to each identified factor.

- Discuss why it is important to consider personal psychological reactions to specific colors when developing color plans.

- Given any room and a specific list of desired visual and psychological effects, select one good color plan that satisfies these requirements.

## Key Terms and Concepts

Psychology of color

Color's dimensions as related to psychological responses

Warm colors

Cool colors

Stimulating colors

Restful colors

## Learning Activities

- Describe the visual and psychological responses associated with both warm and cool colors.
- Discuss the relationship of hue, value, and intensity on psychological reactions.
- Describe the psychological reactions you want to achieve for a specific room. Select a color plan that would create the desired responses.
- Discuss at least four different factors that should be considered when selecting colors to induce specific psychological reactions in a room.
- Select one color you dislike. Describe the emotional effects it would have on you if used in large quantities within your living environment.

## Optional Activities

- Identify your favorite color for an interior plan. Ask five people what emotional reactions they would have if that color were used in their environment. Discuss the differences in the responses.
- View a furnished room for the first time and identify your initial emotional reactions to the colors used. Remain in the room for several minutes or longer and determine if your feelings remain the same.

## Optional Readings

Itten, Johannes. *The Elements of Color.* New York: Van Nostrand Reinhold Co., 1970. Pages 45–48 and 83–90. Very interesting presentation of the psychological and emotional qualities expressed by colors.

Lüscher, Dr. Max. *The Lüscher Color Test.* New York: Pocket Books, 1971. Fascinating book on psychological color testing based on personal color preferences.

Whiton, Sherrill. *Interior Design and Decoration.* Philadelphia: J. B. Lippincott Co., 1974. Pages 451–52. Basic information on the psychology of color-test findings.

# COLOR WITH

# 10

# CONFIDENCE

Color Planning

**Assignments for Unit Ten**

1. Read the Overview, Student Learning Objectives, and Learning Supplement for this unit.

2. Watch Television Program Ten, "Color with Confidence." *Be sure to view this program on a color television set.*

3. Review Part 5 in *Beginnings of Interior Environment,* paying particular attention to pages 105-18.

4. Consider Key Terms and Concepts.

5. Complete the Learning Activities.

6. Review the Student Learning Objectives.

## Overview

Developing a color plan for an entire home or for one room is a challenge. Here you begin to apply in an aesthetically pleasing way what you know about the theory and psychology of color. Remember that a beautiful color scheme is the result of incorporating several important considerations into one plan. For example, a color scheme frequently loses its charm when the family discovers that particular color choices require excessive maintenance. Similarly, a color plan that looks perfect in natural lighting may appear dull or look entirely different under artificial lights.

Even though there is no absolute list of steps to follow when developing color plans, Program Ten suggests one very good system. When this is followed, the final product will be well-designed and will reflect personal preferences as well as the desired mood, theme, or atmosphere.

The planning sequence and completed design is discussed in the program by an interior designer, but any person willing to work and apply these techniques and procedures can create a plan equally attractive and satisfactory.

There are additional points that you may want to consider during initial planning stages. If you have a mobile life style, you may need to select more neutral or versatile colors for the major furniture pieces than if you were developing a plan for a permanent residence. Also, it is a good idea to think through several variations of the basic color scheme with this same furniture. Try to determine the adaptability of these colors to different background areas such as flooring or wall colors.

Solid colors sometimes provide more opportunities for variations in a color plan than do patterned materials. This factor is important not only to those who have mobile life styles, but also to those families preferring to make more frequent changes in their decor. A patterned wall covering, a few new accessories, and a different paint color are a few of the inexpensive yet effective ways to revitalize a room that has relatively simple, understated furniture pieces.

You may be tempted to base your schemes on current color trends or fads. When the market is saturated with products in specific colors, consumers tend to select these colors, not so much because they express personal preferences, but because they are readily available and are marketed to capture the consumer's attention. Keep in mind that, as with all fashions, the popularity of specific colors changes fairly rapidly. All too often, they lose their personal appeal within a very few years. In addition, once a color is no longer "in," it is difficult to find replacements for worn items or new pieces that coordinate with the original color scheme.

To make the most accurate evaluation of your plans before purchasing, you should request loan samples of wall coverings, carpeting, fabrics, and the like. Some retailers allow you to check out a sample directly; others will order a small loan sample for your use. These samples allow you to evaluate colors in the setting in which they will be used, and to determine how all the selections for one room relate to each other.

After you have developed a complete color plan, you may want to divide your purchasing into several budget stages. However, in the months ahead, when you will be ready to buy, some of your original choices could be discontinued. Although it is always possible to find excellent substitutions for your original selections, if there are particular ones you feel you must have, purchase these first.

The development of good color transition from one room to another should always be considered early in the planning stages. The completed home plan in Program Ten shows rooms with very closely related color schemes. Although it is not essential that the colors used throughout a home be this repetitive, adjacent rooms should incorporate some of the same color, including value and intensity variations, so that a rhythmic flow is established.

## Student Learning Objectives

When you complete Unit Ten, you should be able to do the following:

- Identify one of the suggested approaches for developing a color scheme and, applying this approach, suggest a complete color plan for a room.

- Select a room and specify the following functions for the room: desired theme or mood, needed visible changes, and psychological and personal color preferences. Develop a total color plan that satisfies these specified requirements.

- Given a picture of a furnished kitchen, develop a transitional color plan that conforms with the principles of design for an adjacent family room.

- Using established guidelines and criteria, describe a sequential pattern of the development for a color plan for a room.

## Learning Supplement

As you purchase various furnishings for your home, develop a color-swatch file for future reference. This easy-to-carry color resource can be extremely helpful and can prevent color errors when you shop for additional items such as towels and accessories. The samples should be large enough to show all the dominant colors in each major area (wall coverings, flooring, predominant wood tones, and others). The samples should be grouped together to represent each room and attractively arranged on paper or an illustration board. Although a swatch file can be developed on individual boards, it is easier to transport and use if the layouts are connected in some type of notebook, scrapbook, or photographic folder, or with metal rings. Ideally the sample sizes should be proportionate to the way in which they are used in the room.

Collect the samples by saving scraps of wall coverings and fabrics. Paint and wood colors can be applied to small pieces of wood or molding. Most wall paints applied to heavy art paper give the same effect. Drapery and upholstery workrooms will provide you with leftover pieces of your fabrics. When upholstery samples are unavailable, some furniture manufacturers will send you a small sample if you request it by code number. Samples impossible to obtain can often be represented by paint chips.

**Key Terms and Concepts**

Color-plan development steps

Complete color plan

Color fads

Color transition

Swatch file

**Learning Activities**

- Complete Color Cards Eight and Nine in the Student Packet. Follow the directions listed on pages 123 and 124 of your text.

- Select a picture of a furnished room, and discuss the following points in relation to use of color within that room:

  a. Theme or mood
  b. Visual effects (in the room or in specific furnishings) produced by specific values and intensities
  c. Hue, value, and intensity distribution
  d. Possible psychological reactions of those living in the room.

- Define transitional color planning.

- Using pictures of an upholstered sofa and one chair, each in different colors, develop a color plan that successfully incorporates these two pieces into one room.

- Discuss the importance of the five planning steps (presented in the program) in the development of a satisfactory color plan.

**Optional Activities**

- Select two of the methods for developing livable color schemes presented on page 105 of your text, and develop color plans. Evaluate the results according to your personal preferences. (Use color schemes other than the one used for the Color Card Eight assignment.)

■ View the furnishing displays in several department and/or furniture stores, and discuss the current color trends or "fads." Basing your conclusions on your observations and opinions, explain what changes will be seen in popular use within the next three years.

**Optional Readings**

*Better Homes and Gardens Decorating Book,* 3rd edition. Des Moines: Meredith Corporation, 1975. Pages 25–56. Excellent chapter on color elements and planning.

Faulkner, Ray, and Faulkner, Sarah. *Inside Today's Home.* New York: Holt, Rinehart and Winston, 1975. Pages 206–10. Brief, easy-to-understand information on developing color schemes and color's role in reducing dollar expenditure.

Witon, Sherrill. *Interior Design and Decoration.* Philadelphia: J. B. Lippincott Co., 1974. Pages 447–53. Brief but good information on color harmonies and general color planning.

# ENLIGHTEN

**11**

# YOUR HOME

Light Your Designs

**Assignments for Unit Eleven**

1. Read the Overview, Student Learning Objectives, and Learning Supplement for this unit.

2. Watch Television Program Eleven, "Enlighten Your Home."

3. Read pages 80-83 in Part 4 of *Beginnings of Interior Environment.*

4. Consider Key Terms and Concepts.

5. Complete the Learning Activities.

6. Review the Student Learning Objectives.

## Overview

No matter how well a room is decorated, much of its design impact is lost if the lighting throughout is insufficient. Well-planned lighting can make even the modestly decorated home look special. The selection, use, and control of natural daylight and artificial illumination can determine the beauty, safety, and function of an interior environment. Therefore, lighting should be carefully planned and never left as an afterthought in designing.

Lighting needs should be analyzed according to activities that will take place in a particular room. You will find that different rooms require different types and degrees of lighting. Illuminating engineers have found that the proper light for a given task can relax and refresh, while poor or incorrectly planned lighting can cause fatigue and irritation. (See Figure 11.1 in this guide.)

You must take a daytime and night-time inventory of the room's lighting needs, whether you are planning a new house or making changes in an existing one. The mood you wish to create within the room should also be an important consideration in your plan. A mood that is quiet, serene, and restful is easily created with low intensity lighting while a lively, cheerful mood is created with a higher lighting level.

In your plan, you might want to think about visually controlling the size of your room with lighting. If you light up an entire wall with track lighting, the wall will seem to expand, and make the room appear larger. Soft lights tend to minimize the environment and attract attention to the detail within it.

Are you aware that color and texture can affect your lighting plan? A nubby texture such as burlap or grasscloth on a wall will absorb light. A painted surface will reflect light, but notice that a dark, painted surface will absorb more light than a lighter color wall.

Lighting should be balanced in a room the same way that you would balance the visual weight of your furniture. General lighting—the low level that illuminates an entire room—creates the overall lighting mood and meets usual lighting needs. This type of lighting should be evenly distributed. Task lighting—additional illumination for specific activities such as reading or sewing—supplements the general lighting plan. Task lighting is best controlled through dimmers or three-way switches. Accent lighting, used to highlight art objects and paintings or to emphasize wall areas, creates dramatic effects and focuses our attention on interesting areas or objects.

After thinking through your lighting needs, you are ready to select the light fixture for your particular situation. You should be aware that incandescent lighting is most commonly used in residences. Incandescent bulbs cast a yellowish tint and may weaken colors in the blue-violet range. Incandescent bulbs come in wattages from 10 to 300 watts, but it should be noted that wattage is not a measure of the light emitted; rather, it is the amount of electricity going into the light bulb. The amount of light radiated from a bulb is measured in lumens.

Fluorescent lighting is available in tube form and in variations of wattage and color. Fluorescent light is less flexible than incandescent because tubes of different wattages are not interchangeable in the same fixture (the longer the tube, the higher the wattage). However, fluorescent lights give off more light, last longer, and use less energy than incandescent. They produce three to four times the light produced by incandescents of the same wattage, and they last seven to ten times longer than the incandescents. Most fluorescents in use today have a bluish cast that reduces the vitality of warm colors. It is not flattering to complexions, either. However, there are fluorescent lights now that have been "color improved" so that colors look natural. These may be used and blended with incandescent light.

You may have noticed a trend toward lighting that is structural or built in. This type of lighting is a fixture or a unit built directly into a ceiling, wall, window frame, or furniture. The principal advantage of structural lighting is that it offers superior light distribution. It also can be custom built to your requirements and takes up little or no space. Built-in lighting has no cords and actually enhances the architectural character of your home.

If you move frequently or rent, you may want to purchase portable lighting sources. If you do decide to include some structural lighting in a rented dwelling, it is advisable to get the owner's permission in writing before proceeding. However, you can simulate the effect of built-in lighting with portable canister lights or with spotlights that sit on the floor. Track lighting can be attached to walls or the ceiling and taken with you when you leave.

Another alternative for the renter is furniture with built-in lighting. Look for this option when purchasing new furniture or, if you are a competent craftsman, consider adding lighting to furniture you have.

Portable lighting consists of fixtures that you can unplug and move to another room or house. While there is a wide variety of portable fixtures on the market, the most common are table or desk lamps, swag lamps, floor lamps, and some wall lamps. When choosing portable lighting for a particular situation, you should be aware of its value not only as task and accent lighting, but also as a vital decorative accessory. Therefore, consider the theme of the area in which this lighting source will be used.

All lamps must have shades to diffuse light and prevent glare. Lamp shades vary widely in size, color, and translucency, but your choice should suit the scale of your lamp base and be in keeping with the general decorating scheme. The degree of translucency in the shades will be determined by the purpose of the lighting. Lamp shades of a light color provide the best lighting, but more dramatic effects can be achieved if one shade in a room is opaque.

Most of our homes are proof of the lack of planning that goes into a lighting scheme. Electrical outlets and switches are many times placed with little real thought for their use in everyday living. Ideally, there should be at least two outlets on each wall and a switch by every door to control light when you enter.

## Student Learning Objectives

When you complete Unit Eleven, you should be able to do the following:

- Discuss the importance of well-planned lighting as it relates to the function and beauty of a room.

- Identify at least four factors to consider when determining the amount of light needed for a room.

- List and explain two advantages and two disadvantages for both incandescent and fluorescent residential lighting.

- Select a furnished room and activity list and identify the needs for both general and specific task lighting.

## Learning Supplement

In addition, a fact worth noting about incandescent bulbs is that they are either standard or long-life. Long-life bulbs have filaments that are heavier and thus will last longer. However, they also give less light. The long-life bulb will last three times longer, but gives 300 fewer lumens than a standard bulb of the same wattage.

Available, too, are energy-saving bulbs that consume 8 percent less electricity yet provide the same amount of light as do conventional wattage bulbs. They have a higher initial cost, but they are more economical because they use less electricity.

For reading and close work where brightness counts, a standard bulb is the best. But with a difficult-to-reach fixture such as in a stairwell, a long-life bulb is better and far more convenient.

Don't ignore the coating that covers the bulb. The lightly frosted, glare-free, white type are the most efficient, giving off more light than do the heavily frosted bulbs. Clear bulbs work well where they are completely concealed, such as in some ceiling fixtures, because they give off more light than the more attractive coated bulbs.

## Key Terms and Concepts

Contrast
Task lighting

General lighting

Accent lighting

Incandescent

Fluorescent

Architectural lighting

Warm lighting

Cool lighting

Diffusion

## Learning Activities

- Explain how well-planned lighting pertains to a room's function, beauty, and safety.

- Name three types of artificial lighting, and describe a specific use for each type.

- List the benefits of architectural lighting as compared to portable lighting.

- Develop a plan that uses both architectural and portable lighting sources to satisfy the needs of a combination kitchen/family room.

- List several advantages and disadvantages for both incandescent and fluorescent lighting.

## Optional Activities

- When you visit a major department store, notice the use of fluorescent and incandescent lights. Where is one type used almost exclusively? Why?

- Examine the types of lighting fixtures throughout your own home. Do they function as well as you planned? How could you improve the situation?

- How do fine restaurants successfully create mood lighting? Try to determine the techniques employed.

## Optional Readings

Alexander, Mary Jean. *Designing Interior Environment.* New York: Harcourt Brace Jovanovich, Inc., 1972. Pages 86–100 and 105–10. Comprehensive information on the uses and selection criteria for artificial lighting.

Birren, Faber. *Light, Color and Environment.* New York: Van Nostrand Reinhold Co., 1969. Biological and psychological aspects of color, indicating some of the possibilities for manipulation of environment through the use of light and color.

Faulkner, Ray, and Faulkner, Sarah. *Inside Today's Home.* New York: Holt, Rinehart and Winston, 1975. Pages 88–102. Comprehensive, practical information on the selection and placement of artificial lighting; functional and aesthetic uses of artificial light discussed in detail.

## Selection Guide for Incandescent Bulbs
### Reprinted from *Better Homes and Gardens*

| Activity | Recommended Wattage |
|---|---|
| **Reading, writing, sewing:** | |
| Occasional periods | 150 |
| Prolonged periods | 200 or 300 |
| **Grooming:** | |
| Bathroom mirror: | |
| 1 fixture on each side of mirror | 75 or 2 40's |
| 1 fixture over mirror | 150 |
| Bathroom ceiling fixture | 120 |
| **Kitchen work:** | |
| Ceiling fixture (2 or more in large area) | 150 or 200 |
| Fixture over sink | 150 |
| **Shopwork:** | |
| Fixture for workbench | 150 |

## Selection Guide for Fluorescent Tubes

| Activity | Wattage and color |
|---|---|
| **Reading, writing, sewing:** | |
| Occasional periods | 1 40w or 2 20w, WWX or CWX* |
| Prolonged periods | 2 40w or 2 30w, WWX or CWX |
| **Wall lighting:** | |
| Small living area (8 foot minimum) | 2 40w, WWX or CWX |
| Large living area (16 foot minimum) | 4 40w, WWX or CWX |
| **Grooming:** | |
| Bathroom mirror: | |
| 1 fixture on each side of mirror | 2 20w or 2 30w, WWX |
| 1 fixture over mirror | 1 40w, WWX or CWX |
| Bathroom ceiling fixture | 1 40w, WWX |
| Luminous ceiling | 2-foot squares, 2 20w, WWX or CWX |
| | 3-foot squares, 4 30w, WWX or CWX |
| | 4-foot squares, 4 40w, WWX or CWX |

**Kitchen work:**
    Ceiling fixture ............................................. 2 40w or 2 30w, WWX
    Over sink ........................................ 2 40w or 2 30w, WWX, CWX
    Countertop lighting ................... 20w or 40w to fill length, WWX
    Dining area (separate from kitchen) ........ 15 or 20 watts for each
                       30 inches of longest dimension of room area, WWX

**Home workshop:** ....................................... 2 40w, CW, CWX, WWX

*WWX—warm white deluxe, CWX—cool white deluxe, CW—cool white
**Note:** These requirements vary according to room color. In general, the lighter the color, the higher the reflectance and the greater the utilization of light.

Figure 11.1—Selection Guides for Incandescent and Fluorescent Bulbs. © Copyright Meredith Corporation, 1975. All rights reserved.

# SPACE PLANNING

## 12

## PLANNING

Forms In Space

**Assignments for Unit Twelve**

1. Read the Overview and Student Learning Objectives for this unit.

2. Watch Television Program Twelve, "Space Planning."

3. Read pages 255-74 in Part 9 of *Beginnings of Interior Environment.*

4. Review Part 4 of your text and relate it specifically to use of space, activity planning, and furniture arrangement.

5. Consider Key Terms and Concepts.

6. Complete the Learning Activities.

7. Review the Student Learning Objectives.

## Overview

Careful planning of the available space within a room is a challenging task in interior design. Space plans involve not only the division and allocation of space, but also the direction and flow of traffic, activity planning, and well-thought-out furniture-arrangement plans. An accurate assessment of family needs and the incorporation of these needs into a comprehensive plan insure that a room will function well.

A complete furniture-arrangement plan, created in part through a careful examination of your needs and resources, and the principles of design, is essential to a well-designed room and a total interior plan. But before determining an arrangement plan, you need to study the interior space of the room or rooms, and make a scale floor-plan drawing. Use an architectural scale to chart dimensions, accesses, openings, electrical outlets, and other fixed architectural features, and include these features in your plan as well. (A review of Unit Six would be helpful.)

As you work with the spaces within your home, you will find that rooms with similar dimensions may give very different space impressions. These impressions are directly related to the main entrance of the room and it is from this point that the room will be viewed most often. How spacious or how small the space seems is related to how far or near the opposite wall is to the room's doorway. The sizes and placement of windows and other openings should be considered as well, because the perspective of the area is dependent upon all these factors.

After you have drawn your floor plan, divide the space into general activity areas and locate traffic patterns. Traffic lanes are the areas that need to be left open and unencumbered by furniture.

Usually, the traffic patterns developed in each room subdivide the space into distinct and obvious zones. When this happens, the task of activity planning is simplified considerably. The purpose of activity planning is to chart the intended use of space and furniture requirements within a room. Each activity area demands individualized study in which the needs of those persons using the space influence the choice of furniture, color, and materials. In this stage of planning, it is necessary to allow enough room for each activity that will take place within the room. The minimum clearances given on page 267 in your text will be beneficial in planning your activity spaces. The job of matching the space requirement of each activity to the space available should be simpler. At times an area may be large enough to allow for the separation of all activities; in other spaces, activities must overlap and rooms must meet a variety of purposes.

Functional planning is of the utmost importance in any design situation, but once you have carefully considered and logically planned these aspects, you can turn your attention to aesthetics. The most important factors at this point include the relationship of the scale of furnishings to the available space, the contrast of horizontal and vertical elements, and the harmonious composition of furniture groupings.

Your text offers several solutions to design problems that arise in arranging space. The details related pertain to achieving desired effects, such as a more spacious or more intimate feeling within a room.

Effective space planning and functional furniture arrangement deserves early and careful study, particularly in regard to your family's life style. Keep in mind that there is no one way to arrange a space, that it is best to determine what is important to you and your family and which plan allows the most effective use of the available space.

**Student Learning Objectives**

When you complete Unit Twelve, you should be able to do the following:

■ Define the general goal of space planning.

■ List at least five functional considerations for furniture arrangement, and explain how to evaluate each during the planning stage.

■ Identify and discuss the primary steps required to correctly complete a furniture arrangement plan.

■ Make up a list of the functions and areas of activity for a given floor plan. Establish furniture needs, and develop a furniture-arrangement plan satisfying the identified requirements.

■ Using the principles of design, evaluate the floor and wall compositions of a specified furnished room. Suggest changes in the plan that would improve the total design.

**Key Terms and Concepts**

Space planning

Space impression

Minimum clearances

Activity planning

Activity areas

Traffic patterns

**Learning Activities**

■ Make a list of ten guidelines given in your text, and apply them to the arrangement of furniture and space use in your own home.

- Choose a room in your home that must function for several purposes. Suggest other ways you might make this room more flexible.

- Your text has listed some ways that a room may be made to appear larger. Using color, fabrics, furniture, and accessories, how would you select, apply, and arrange these items to solve a space problem?

- Examine one room in your home. Evaluate the floor and wall compositions, keeping in mind the design principles and criteria given in the program and text. Make suggestions for improving the total design.

## Optional Activities

- When visiting friends' homes, touring model homes, or observing room settings in periodicals, determine whether or not space has been used effectively.

- Evaluate your own home and its functional qualities. Are there good traffic patterns? Does the furniture need rearranging? Are the activity areas well-planned for maximum use?

## Optional Readings

Faulkner, Ray, and Faulkner, Sarah. *Inside Today's Home.* New York: Holt, Rinehart and Winston, 1975. Pages 3–136. Discussion of interior space usage.

Sulahria, Julie, and Diamond, Ruby. *Inside Design: Creating Your Environment.* San Francisco: Canfield Press, 1977. Pages 65–84. Evaluation of various space divisions within a home.

# MAKE YOUR OWN

## 13

# ARRANGEMENT

Design in Compact Areas

**Assignments for Unit Thirteen**

1. Read the Overview, Student Learning Objectives, and Learning Supplement for this unit.

2. Watch Television Program Thirteen, "Make Your Own Arrangement."

3. Review pages 258-263 in Part 9 of *Beginnings of Interior Environment.*

4. Consider Key Terms and Concepts.

5. Complete the Learning Activities.

6. Review the Student Learning Objectives.

## Overview

Some unique spaces that offer a real challenge to the designer include small apartments, compact dwellings such as condominiums, townhomes, mobile homes, and even the smaller alcoves and rooms of a regular-sized home. These so-called problem areas usually must serve a variety of purposes, but the available space is limited—and therein lies the problem. But with careful furniture arrangement and the use of furniture that is flexible and adaptable, you can design a satisfactory environment in these small areas. This unit, then, uses the techniques suggested in Unit Twelve, "Space Planning," and applies them to smaller areas.

Particularly in a smaller area is it important to create a plan and follow it. After you have established family needs, take one room at a time and analyze its anticipated uses. At this point it is wise to determine alternative arrangement plans. Even though you feel you have developed the best furniture arrangement possible for that particular area, try to visualize the room used in other situations. Often, a simple rearrangement will allow a room to function better daytime *and* night-time, in all seasons, and for a wide variety of activities, from family use to formal entertaining.

Through wise planning and precise furnishing, you can expand the limited space at hand and increase its usefulness. Keep in mind that good planning requires practicality, flexibility, a working knowledge of the design elements, and (especially) accurate measurements. Because these areas are small, it is important that all furnishings, current and anticipated, fit the available space and meet the needs of the individuals using that space. (Review pages 267-68 in your text for the minimum clearances necessary in a functional room.)

Furniture pieces should also be adaptable and preferably portable to suit a number of needs throughout the overall design. For example, one set of dining chairs could serve several functions. In addition to their primary function, they could be deployed throughout the home as desk chairs, bedroom accessories, or additional seating in a conversation area. This practice will not only save money, but will also conserve valuable space. Therefore, when planning and selecting furniture for a small area, choose pieces that can be regrouped easily in compatible arrangements and that are scaled to fit the other design components within that same plan. As a bonus, adaptable and flexible furniture pieces are assets to individuals who have mobile life styles. These furniture pieces can be moved easily, not only from room to room, but also from home to home.

Your text offers guidelines and suggestions for arranging furniture in specific rooms. (Refer to pages 258-69 and Part 10.) Adapt these guidelines to your own smaller rooms and, at the same time, blend function with beauty and comfort.

In many small dwellings, it will be up to you to define living zones by "visually" dividing your space to suit your way of life. Furniture arrangement can easily do this for you. Setting a sofa, several chairs, and a table on an area rug can tie them together so that they act as a unit even though they are not surrounded by four walls. Pieces of furniture, such as bookcases, separate and define space and can divide a room. If you so choose, forget the traditional designations of living room or dining room. Do not allow convention to dictate how you can rearrange available space to suit your life style and needs. However, do not overlook the need for privacy in small dwellings.

## Student Learning Objectives

When you complete Unit Thirteen, you should be able to do the following:

- List the required furniture for a specific room and its proposed activities. Applying the principles of design, develop two alternate furniture arrangements satisfying the needs of each activity.

- Explain at least three considerations to apply when planning furniture arrangements for a small living room/bedroom.

- Discuss the importance of developing adaptable furnishing plans for mobile life styles. Explain at least five selection factors to help insure that established furnishings will adapt to new dwellings.

- Select a furnished room and develop a three-segment purchase plan for all the furnishings. Discuss how segments one and two will be completed to satisfy functional and aesthetic criteria.

- List at least five low-cost ideas that may be incorporated to reduce the cost of specific furniture pieces for one room.

## Learning Supplement

As you know, it is best to have a long-term plan that spells out your furniture needs. Make a plan for each room of your apartment or house. Include all necessary furniture even though you may not purchase it all at once. In this way you can get a complete picture of your needs, and you will be able to budget accordingly.

Once you have developed a good, overall plan, you can establish priorities and plan those items you will add as your budget allows. A plan such as this will help you avoid hasty, unwise purchases.

The basics—furnishings that provide comfort and convenience—should be budgeted first. Items that you want but that are not necessary can be postponed.

The logical progression in developing a budget with your plan in mind is from necessities to secondary furnishings to the final stage and the finishing touches. Don't forget to include maintenance and refurbishing in your budget.

It is important that you get the most for your money, and budget-expanding ideas can help you stretch each dollar. Many of these ideas involve using your creativity, time, and energy while others depend upon forethought and attention to details. Planning for annual sale periods and visiting garage sales and auctions are ways to save money. If you buy temporary furniture to "fill-in," try to plan secondary uses for it. For example, a less expensive sofa table might become a desk in a child's room later. Director's chairs are inexpensive and can be used in a living room temporarily, then moved to the patio.

## Key Terms and Concepts

Flexible planning

Alternative furniture arrangements

Adaptable furnishings

Townhome

Condominium

Living zones

"Visually" dividing space

"Fill-in" furniture

## Learning Activities

- Complete the assignment on pages 267-69 in your text. See the Student Packet for duplicates of the templates, living room plans, etc., mentioned in the text assignment. Note that some of these same activity cards (specifically "Living Room One," "Living Room Two," "Living-Dining Room Three," "Child's Bedroom Four," and the templates) will also be used in later assignments. It is recommended, therefore, that you either copy these plans on additional graph paper or work with them in such a way that they can be used again.

- Incorporate into your resource file illustrations of low-cost furniture pieces that could work well in most design plans.

## Optional Activities

- Evaluate the importance of your time and abilities with reference to planning and implementing a long-range furnishing plan. How might you be able to stretch your budget or make your plan function better during the various purchasing stages?

- Consider the importance of developing adaptable furnishing plans for mobile life styles. List and explain five selection factors that help insure the adaptability of furnishings to new dwellings.

## Optional Readings

*Better Homes and Gardens Decorating Book,* 3rd edition. Des Moines: Meredith Corporation, 1975. Pages 89–120; pages 249–80; and pages 345–76. Excellent source of additional guidelines for furniture arrangement in small areas.

Faulkner, Ray, and Faulkner, Sarah. *Inside Today's Home.* New York: Holt, Rinehart and Winston, 1975. Pages 410–21. Good information on planned buying and arranging furniture for activities. Special selection on furniture sizes and clearance spaces.

Whiton, Sherrill. *Interior Design and Decoration.* Philadelphia: J. B. Lippincott Co., 1974. Pages 645–51. Excellent information on planning furniture arrangement based on needs. Space organization emphasized.

# TREAD

## SOFTLY

**14**

Floor Coverings (Part 1)

**Assignments for Unit Fourteen**

1. Read the Overview, Student Learning Objectives, and Learning Supplement for this unit.

2. Watch Television Program Fourteen, "Tread Softly."

3. Read pages 184-201 of Part 7 in *Beginnings of Interior Environment*.

4. Consider Key Terms and Concepts.

5. Complete the Learning Activities.

6. Review Student Learning Objectives.

## Overview

Throughout history, people have covered the hard floors of their homes with various types of softer coverings for needed warmth, beauty, and comfort. Soft floor coverings are used today, too, for those same purposes as well as to unify rooms, create an illusion of spaciousness, or lend a feeling of closeness or intimacy.

Keep in mind that it is possible to add definite characteristics to a space by choosing a soft covering carefully. Size, color, texture, and pattern can affect the style of your room. Even the amount of floor that you cover can emphasize the mood or theme you are trying to set, as well as increase or decrease the apparent size of the room. For example, if you are trying to achieve a feeling of spaciousness, choose a light, solid-color wall-to-wall carpeting. And if it is extended throughout adjoining areas, that same wall-to-wall carpeting will create a look of unity.

Rugs and carpets are distinguished from each other by size. Rugs come in precut, specific sizes and shapes, have finished edges, and can be moved easily from room to room or home to home. Carpets are made by the yard and are usually tacked down around the baseboards for permanent installation. A room-size rug can create an effect similar to wall-to-wall carpeting and could be more practical for some people who move often.

The fibers most commonly used for soft floor coverings are nylon, acrylic, polyester, olefin, and wool. For special purposes, silk, grass, rush, cotton, and other plant fibers such as sisal, jute, and even strips of paper are sometimes used. At one time, wool was the major carpet and rug fiber, but the popularity of manmade fibers, the diminishing sources of good carpet wools, and the resulting high cost has led to a decline in wool usage. Nylon is now the chief carpet fiber, followed by acrylics, polyesters, and olefins.

There are four major methods of constructing a machine-made carpet or rug: tufting, weaving, knitting, and needlepunching. (Review the construction methods as explained in pages 188-90 in your text.) However, much more emphasis is placed on the fiber content and brand name of a carpet than on the type of construction employed. But this does not minimize the fact that consumer knowledge of carpet and rug construction can facilitate the best selection.

Handmade rugs include the beautiful Oriental rugs from the Orient or Near East as well as folk, ethnic, or peasant rugs. Some of the first people to make rugs by hand were shepherds and nomads, and today's modern methods of weaving with power looms are based on the ancient hand methods. Machine-made rugs that resemble the genuine handmade Oriental rug are constructed on powered Jacquard looms and are called domestic or American Orientals. They must be clearly labeled to distinguish them from the genuine Oriental rugs.

The texture and design of soft floor coverings are created during construction by varying the color and types of yarn used or by using a pattern attachment. After the floor covering has been constructed, the pattern, design, and texture can be changed by printing, carving, or sculpting the surface. In addition, settings can be varied on the tufting machine so that the carpeting can be made with both cut pile and uncut loop pile for a wide range of design effects. The amount of twist and the length of the pile also dictate the carpet style and its eventual use.

A carpet underlay or "use cushion" will increase durability, improve the effectiveness of the vacuum cleaner in removing dirt from the flooring, and make the carpet a more pleasant walking surface. The text gives excellent information about the various types available. Remember that your carpet is only as good as the cushion beneath it.

Carpet manufacturers recommend that a vacuum cleaner be used twice a week in most areas, and daily in areas that receive heavy traffic. Spots and stains should be removed as soon as possible. If information on stain removal is not included on the carpet's label and is unavailable from the source of purchase, you may write the Carpet and Rug Institute in Dalton, Georgia, and ask for a copy of the booklet, "How to Care for Your Carpets and Rugs."

Whatever type of carpeting or rug you choose, plan carefully and early to secure the effect and quality suited to your specific purpose. Make sure that your choice is an integral element that complements the overall design of your home.


**Student Learning Objectives**

When you complete Unit Fourteen, you should be able to do the following:

- List two possible reasons for selecting each of the following types of soft surface floor coverings: wall-to-wall carpet, room-size or large rugs, small area or accent rugs.

- Identify at least four factors used to evaluate the quality of carpeting. Explain how to evaluate a given piece of carpeting in relation to each factor.

- Identify one advantage and one disadvantage for each of the following types of fibers used in carpets: wool, nylon, acrylic, polyester, olefin.

- Describe two specific types of handmade rugs.

- List at least three functions of carpet underlay.

- Explain at least five specific factors a consumer can consider when selecting carpeting to prevent future disappointments.

## Learning Supplement

When you shop for quality carpeting or rugs, do not overlook one very important consumer aid—the label. Federal regulations require that soft floor coverings be labeled to provide the following information: the country of origin, the manufacturer's name or code number, the generic names of the face fibers (those on the surface only) used, and the percentage of each if over 5 percent. Even though it is not required by law, the label should also list the pattern name, color, cleaning instructions, and special treatments such as mothproofing or antistatic that have been applied. Also, all carpets now on the market must pass a government test for flame retardancy.

Use your fingers to determine a carpet's or rug's quality. Examine the piece for density of pile, amount of twist in the yarn, and overall texture. Look for the term "autoclave heat set" on the label of a synthetic, cut pile carpet as a further indication of quality. Compare several examples of carpeting that have the same fiber content and style characteristics. And always deal with a reputable retail firm.

## Key Terms and Concepts

Pile density

Pile depth

Autoclave heat set

Twist

Carpet underlay

Face fibers

Splush

Polyester

Nylon

Acrylic

Olefin

Tufting

"Bottoms out"

## Learning Activities

■ Select a soft floor covering that would exemplify a formal mood in a dining room and suit the style of furniture chosen. What particular surface characteristics and design features might be desirable?

■ Compare the aesthetic and functional properties of various soft floor covering fibers by making a carpet/rug analysis chart. The following headings are suggested:

| Fiber and Properties | Area Where Used | Advantages Disadvantages | Construction | Pile/ Density | Furniture Style |
|---|---|---|---|---|---|
| | | | | | |

On your chart, do the following as well:

a. List properties of each carpet fiber and suggest uses. (What are the advantages and disadvantages of each fiber?)
b. Describe the construction techniques most appropriate for the fiber and its intended use.
c. Indicate pile height and density that would be most suitable for a particular fiber and area.
d. Select a carpet style for these criteria, and indicate what furnishings would complement the picture.

## Optional Activities

- For a beneficial addition to your resource file, you may want to consider the following booklet: *A Consumer Guide to Carpet.* This publication is easy to read and contains valuable consumer information. Write to: Allied Chemical Corporation, Fibers Division, Contract Department, 1 Times Square, New York, New York 10036.

- Visit a small carpet mill if there is one nearby. Discuss different construction techniques with the owner or manager. Ask to see the carpet primary backing before any construction occurs.

## Optional Readings

*Better Homes and Gardens Decorating Book,* 3rd Edition. Des Moines: Meredith Corporation, 1975. Pages 150–52. Comprehensive and descriptive fiber chart for soft floor covering. Chart showing how to estimate carpet yardage.

Collins, Peggie Varney, and Collins, Shirley Wright. *Putting It All Together: A Consumer's Guide to Home Furnishings.* New York: Charles Scribner's Sons, 1977. Pages 31–45. Excellent consumer information on soft floor coverings.

Whiton, Sherrill. *Interior Design and Decoration.* Philadelphia: J. B. Lippincott Co., 1974. Pages 475–501. Good overview of soft floor coverings, including installation of various types. Has section on carpets and rugs used as wall coverings. Excellent section on dyeing processes.

# BENEATH YOUR FEET

## 15

Floor Coverings (Part 2)

**Assignments for Unit Fifteen**

1. Read the Overview, Student Learning Objectives, and Learning Supplement for this unit.

2. Watch Television Program Fifteen, "Beneath Your Feet."

3. Read pages 171-84 of Part 7 in *Beginnings of Interior Environment*.

4. Review Part 4 of the text and relate it to the selection and application of floor coverings.

5. Consider Key Terms and Concepts.

6. Complete the Learning Activities.

7. Review the Student Learning Objectives.

## Overview

Technology has produced such a wide variety of new materials and has improved the familiar ones in so many ways that a revival of hard-surface flooring has swept through the country during the past fifteen years. Today most residential interiors include at least one type of resilient, nonresilient, or wood floor covering.

Floors contribute to the expressive character of an entire house. They can define and separate areas, suggest traffic patterns, and be as dominant or unobtrusive as desired. An undemanding, plain surface can be a passive yet unifying base for furniture, but a bold pattern can call attention to the floor and set the theme for which the space was planned. In fact, space planning can be intensified through the creative use of floor materials.

Careful planning and forethought should be emphasized in applying the principles of design to floors. And the selections of resilient, nonresilient, and wood floorings should be based on evaluations of the product's functional characteristics, maintenance requirements, and aesthetic qualities in relation to overall cost. Some points to consider before purchasing a particular covering might be the character and beauty of the floor-covering material itself; the effect of the covering in the area for which it is being considered; and the relation of all the floors in the home to one another and to the design of the entire house. The overwhelming variety of types, colors, textures, and patterns of floor coverings can make it difficult to find the perfect floor covering if you do not have at least a slight idea of the functional and aesthetic qualities your floor covering should have.

Keep in mind the interrelationship of color, texture, and pattern during your examination of floor materials. When applied to coverings, these elements should suggest the function; in other words, the floor should look as if it were meant to be walked on. Pronounced three-dimensional or naturalistic designs might not be appealing at all for a walking area.

Although most people evaluate floor coverings in very small samples and at close range, the effect that large areas and viewing from a distance play in the perception of any design should not be overlooked. Some patterns, when repeated over a large area, become overwhelming. In contrast, some small repeat patterns tend to blend together and create the illusion of texture rather than pattern. Color in a small pattern may also be changed when this blending occurs.

Your text offers solutions to design problems that may arise in choosing hard-surface flooring. It emphasizes the use of particular materials to achieve themes or moods, the suitability of material to the function of a room or area, the initial cost, and the cost of maintenance. Refer to the chart on pages 172-81 of your text for a comprehensive, descriptive guide to hard-surface flooring.

Note that the matter of suitable floors and floor coverings deserves early and careful attention in your overall design plan. Flooring may consist of concrete slab or wooden floors supported by joists (parallel timbers that hold up the planks of the floor). Both may be covered with hard-surface flooring, but there may be some limitations in installation procedures. Possible limitations and problems of installation should be discussed with a professional in the field of hard-surface flooring before a definite selection is made.

Some important factors to consider when choosing suitable floor coverings for your home would be durability, resiliency, and economy of upkeep. For example, floor materials that resist stains and bleaches or do not absorb liquids and dirt are easier to maintain than others. Additional factors include warmth, sound absorption, and light reflection. Appearance is, of course, also important. Keep in mind that practicality and cost should not outweigh aesthetics when choosing a resilient or nonresilient flooring. It is still true that there is yet no one flooring material that is perfect in every respect, so it is sensible to decide which factors are most important to you and which compromises are necessary.

## Student Learning Objectives

When you complete Unit Fifteen, you should be able to do the following:

- Discuss the functional and maintenance characteristics for four specified hard-surface floor coverings.

- List two advantages and two disadvantages for both nonresilient and resilient floor coverings.

- Explain the differences between sheet vinyl and cushioned no-wax sheet vinyl, and discuss several factors that, when considered, would help insure the satisfaction of a consumer selecting one of these products for a kitchen.

- Describe at least four different types of wood flooring, and identify an appropriate room theme or mood for each type.

- Analyze the effect of plastic and acrylic impregnation on wood flooring today.

- Given a house plan, select floor coverings for each room to provide for ease of maintenance, function, economy of resources, and desired aesthetic qualities.

## Learning Supplement

One of the most important yet overlooked aspects of floor covering is how it feels when you walk on it. A wood parquet floor with a wire brush finish may look beautiful and help emphasize the mood or theme of a room, but it would provide little comfort for bare feet. Also, it is important to consider the sensory differences when combining one or more types of hard-surface floorings. When you walk from a soft, cushioned vinyl floor to a dense, nonresilient ceramic tile, you definitely notice a change in sounds, comfort, and even temperature. Try to insure that the flooring you eventually choose is comfortable and easy on your feet as well as attractive and practical.

**Key Terms and Concepts**

Hard-surface flooring

Resilient flooring

Nonresilient flooring

Ceramic

Masonry

Wood parquet

Quarry tile

Glaze

**Learning Activities**

■ Select a hard-surface floor covering that would be suitable in establishing an informal, country mood. What surface characteristics are desirable?

■ Compare the aesthetic and functional properties of one natural and one synthetic hard-surface floor covering of your choice. List their properties and possible uses in a home.

■ Describe ways that resilient and nonresilient flooring may be used in combination with soft floor covering.

■ List advantages and disadvantages of ceramic tile.

**Optional Activities**

■ Add to your resource file of interior design ideas a section on hard-surface floor coverings. Use brochures collected from retail stores. Select several types of flooring, and label specific characteristics you find attractive.

■ Visit a local retail outlet that features a variety of hard-surface flooring. Compare types of hard-surface floor coverings with regard to aesthetic and functional properties as well as cost.

■ Select a ceramic tile pattern, and arrange a scheme that would be compatible with an existing resilient floor covering and soft floor covering. Describe the mood that will result.

**Optional Readings**

*Better Homes and Gardens Decorating Book.* 3rd Edition. Des Moines: Meredith Corporation, 1975. Pages 137–152. Excellent chart describing characteristics, advantages, disadvantages, and maintenance of floor coverings. Section included on estimating yardage.

Collins, Peggie Varney, and Collins, Shirley Wright. *Putting It All Together: A Consumer's Guide to Home Furnishings.* New York: Charles Scribner's Sons, 1977. Pages 46–57. Excellent consumer information on hard-surface flooring.

Sulahria, Julie, and Diamond, Ruby. *Inside Design: Creating Your Environment.* San Francisco: Canfield Press, 1977. Pages 203–208. General classifications and descriptions—not extensive. Some information on wood flooring.

Whiton, Sherrill. *Interior Design and Decoration.* Philadelphia: J. B. Lippincott Co., 1974. Pages 488–490. Information on resilient and nonresilient floor covering. Introduces cork and metal.

# FROM FIBER

## 16

# TO FABRIC

## Finding a Practical Fabric

**Assignments for Unit Sixteen**

1. Read the Overview and Student Learning Objectives for this unit.

2. Watch Television Program Sixteen, "From Fiber to Fabric."

3. Read pages 137-67 in Part 6 of *Beginnings of Interior Environment.* Pay particular attention to pages 137-49 and 157-67.

4. Consider Key Terms and Concepts.

5. Complete the Learning Activities.

6. Review the Student Learning Objectives.

## Overview

Often a consumer will select a beautiful fabric for use as window treatment, upholstery goods, household linen, or accessory but give little or no attention to the fabric's functional qualities. Whether or not a fabric is durable or easy to maintain usually influences a homeowner's long-term satisfaction with that textile.

While Unit Seventeen pertains to the selection and coordination of fabrics, this lesson will help you to determine and evaluate the functional qualities of fabrics used as window treatments and upholstery materials. (This same consumer information can be used when evaluating textiles for other uses in an interior environment.) When it is time to make your fabric selection, it is essential that you know how to interpret information on labels, learn to see quality, and ask retailers appropriate questions.

Because there is no fabric that works perfectly in all situations, your evaluations should always be made in relation to the product's intended use. For example, a fabric that functions beautifully as a window treatment may be inappropriate for use as upholstery. But another could be highly serviceable in both functions.

The primary factors that determine the functional qualities of fabrics are fiber content, type of construction, and additional processes and finishes that can enhance both the functional and the decorative properties of the completed goods. These can determine such things as stability, color permanency, required maintenance, and resistance to abrasion, sun, and insects. Usually a combination of all of these factors dictates the final characteristics of a textile, so it is important to evaluate all aspects of a fabric simultaneously.

Your textbook discusses the primary characteristics and uses for the most common fibers found in interior textiles. However, you may find it helpful to refer to a textile textbook for additional and specific information. For example, did you know that prolonged exposure the sunlight can damage and cause yellowing in cotton fibers?

The fiber content of a fabric may be included on a manufacturer's label. When a fiber blend is used, the exact content of each fiber is usually expressed in percentages. Fabrics consisting of man-made fibers will list the fibers by generic names (polyester, acetate, rayon, etc.) and may also include the manufacturer's registered trade name for the specific fibers. For example, Dacron is a manufacturer's trade name for a polyester fiber. But when a fabric is a blend of several fibers, each fiber imparts its own special functional and aesthetic characteristics. Combining polyester with cotton, for instance, produces a fabric that has the aesthetic qualities of natural cotton and the strength, wrinkle resistance, and ease of maintenance characteristic of polyester.

Although there are many different processes by which fibers or yarns can be made into fabric, such as knitting and felting, the usual method is weaving. The more common weaves are: plain, basket, twill, satin, tapestry, pile, and leno. Each type offers distinct aesthetic and functional qualities.

Occasionally the manufacturer's label will provide information about chemical or mechanical processes used to add color or pattern to a fabric. You may also note a manufacturer's guarantee pertaining to color permanency. When no printed information is provided, this aspect of fabric quality is perhaps the most difficult to evaluate. Carefully inspect the individual fibers and yarns and the fabric back to determine the degree of color penetration. Complete color penetration through the fibers is extremely important in fabrics that will receive hard wear. A second simple test is to check for "color crocking" by rubbing the fabric surface against a lighter-colored fabric. The lighter fabric should not pick up any color.

Special finishes used to enhance a fabric's decorative and functional properties are often listed on the label by description or a registered trademark. These include special processes that provide resistance to insects, mildew, shrinkage, wrinkling, fire, and soiling. In addition, antiseptic finishes reduce the tendency of bacteria growth and absorption of odors. Antistatic finishes prevent the accumulation of static electricity. However, a finish that adds one valuable characteristic, may at the same time reduce another desired property. For example, a finish added to increase the body and draping quality of a fabric may ultimately cause that fabric to change color or to yellow. Keep in mind that some finishes, such as a soil-resistant one, may be removed through normal cleaning processes, and you may or may not be able to replace them.

As you evaluate the functional characteristics of a certain fiber content, construction, and finishing process, consider too the desired aesthetic qualities. Many times you will have to make value judgments based on the criteria most important to you and your family.


**Student Learning Objectives**

When you complete Unit Sixteen, you should be able to do the following:

- Identify the functional and aesthetic characteristics of two natural and two man-made fibers. Explain how to evaluate those characteristics when planning fabric use for interiors.

- Describe the visual appearance of a basket-weave fabric and a twill-weave fabric. Discuss the characteristics of each fabric that would make it a good choice for an upholstered chair receiving hard wear.

- Identify any three functional finishes used on interior fabrics, and discuss the importance of each in relation to interior application.

- Given a textile label, analyze the significance of all given information. Suggest additional information that would help the consumer make the best selection for intended use.

- Given a sample of a printed fabric and label, explain how to evaluate the functional qualities of the fabric in relation to its fiber content, weave, print process, and finish.

## Key Terms and Concepts

Natural fiber

Man-made fiber

Generic name

Trade name

Types of weaves

Dyeing processes: solution, stock, yarn, piece

Hand printing

Mechanical printing

Traditional fabric finishes

Color crocking

## Learning Activities

- List one functional and one aesthetic characteristic for each of the following fibers: linen, cotton, nylon, polyester, acetate, acrylic.

- Identify the following fabric weaves and explain the characteristics for each that would indicate its durability as an upholstery fabric: plain weave, twill weave, satin weave, basket weave.

- Discuss the importance of evaluating the fiber content, construction, and finishing processes of a fabric when determining its functional characteristics.

- Name three fabric finishes that would improve the functional qualities of an upholstered fabric.

- Select one fabric, and explain how to evaluate its potential for use as a window treatment.

- Evaluate the information on an upholstery-fabric label. Determine the label's usefulness in defining the functional properties of the fabric. List at least two additional items that would help in an evaluation of the fabric.

**Optional Activity**

■ Ask a friend to identify an upholstery or a window-treatment fabric that lacks desired functional properties. Determine why the fabric was unsatisfactory, and explain how to prevent a recurrence of this same problem.

**Optional Readings**

Collins, Peggie Varney, and Collins, Shirley Wright. *Putting It All Together: A Consumer's Guide to Home Furnishings.* New York: Charles Scribner's Sons, 1977. Pages 1–30 and 124–25. Excellent consumer information related to the evaluation of functional characteristics of fabrics.

Faulkner, Ray, and Faulkner, Sarah. *Inside Today's Home.* New York: Holt, Rinehart and Winston, 1975. Pages 268–82. Comprehensive information on fibers, fabric construction, and finishing processes. Good chart illustrating functional and aesthetic properties of fabrics.

*Guide to Man-made Fibers.* Washington, D.C.: Man-made Fibers Producers Association, Inc., 1977. Well-written information on the production of man-made fibers. Excellent charts illustrating major uses and characteristics of man-made fibers.

# FINISHING

## 17

# WITH FABRIC

## Many Guidelines to Success

**Assignments for Unit Seventeen**

1. Read the Overview, Student Learning Objectives, and Learning Supplement for this unit.

2. Watch Television Program Seventeen, "Finishing With Fabric." Review Part 6 of *Beginnings of Interior Environment*. Pay particular attention to pages 149-67 for this unit.

3. Consider Key Terms and Concepts.

4. Complete the Learning Activities.

5. Review the Student Learning Objectives.

## Overview

Stop and think just how dull and uninteresting most rooms would be without the use of fabrics. Fabrics are the most versatile and effective medium for incorporating texture, color, and pattern into a room's design. Although fabrics are most commonly used for upholstery and window treatments, your text describes selection criteria for other principal decorative uses. In addition to those listed, fabrics may be effectively used for accessories such as table covers, framed fabric "pictures," pillows, and many more.

The tremendous variety of types, colors, textures, and patterns makes it possible to find the "perfect" fabric. At the same time, the large number from which to choose may lead to confusion and frustration unless you know what characteristics you want. This unit presents a number of guidelines to help you select the right fabric. Suggestions in this study guide, the text, and television program form a strong framework for your fabric decisions.

Keep in mind the interrelationship of color, texture, and pattern when you are evaluating a fabric. For example, a blue color in a shiny, light-reflective fabric will usually appear lighter in color than will the same color in a coarse, nubby texture. And a large-scale pattern will often appear even larger and heavier if the color is intense rather than subdued.

Different types of light affect color as well, so all fabrics should be carefully evaluated in both the natural and the artificial light in which they will be seen within a specific room. When selecting sheer curtain or drapery fabric, be sure to allow the natural light to filter through the sample. You will then be able to determine if the color of the fabric, or even the light entering the room, is changed.

Although most people evaluate fabric at a close range, the effect that viewing at a distance plays in design perception should not be overlooked. If fabric is being selected for textural interest, remember that from a distance some textures become almost invisible. Small repeat patterns frequently blend together or into the background, which then creates an illusion of texture rather than pattern. In addition, this occurrence may change the overall color of the fabric. When viewed from a distance, for example, a small blue-and-red check sometimes appears as a textural purple fabric.

All fabrics used within one room should relate to or even set the mood or theme of the room. Although it is beyond the scope of this lesson to identify all the fabric possibilities for various room themes, it is important that you develop an awareness of the colors, textures, and patterns that create or enhance specific themes or moods. Learn to identify some of the more common types. Using descriptive adjectives for various fabrics, such as *coarse, nubby, informal, formal,* and *elegant* can also be helpful when you select fabrics to express a mood within one room.

Contemporary fabrics frequently depend on color and texture for interest. When pattern is incorporated, it is usually a geometric or abstract design. The degree of formality or informality may be determined by the specific color and type of textural interest selected. For example, a coarse homespun fabric in an earthy brown will "feel" more informal than a fine textural linen in a light blue—yet both could reflect a contemporary flavor. While a few fabrics lend themselves to both contemporary and traditional themes, brocade, damask, silk, needlepoint, satin, and similar fabrics are more suitable for a formal, traditional look. Traditional informality can be beautifully expressed with fabrics such as chintz, muslin, crewel, and printed and checked cottons.

When coordinating patterns to be used in one room, apply the principles of design and evaluate each pattern as it relates to the others and to the room as a whole. Your text provides excellent guidelines for selecting patterns to use singly or mixed with others in one room. When you are learning how to coordinate your selections, remember (1) that well-chosen geometrics can usually be combined with all other design types, (2) that two geometrics can be used together, and (3) that it is more difficult to create satisfactory combinations when you use two or more naturalistic or stylized designs within one room. Also, attempting to match a color in a patterned fabric can lead to a "too decorated" look or may appear too intense in the room. A blend in color relationships offers the best results.

Your text includes some design problems that can be solved by well-considered fabric choices. In addition, understanding the importance of the elements and principles of design as related to fabric selection will provide you with an increased ability to solve many other design problems.

Creating a visual flow or transition throughout a home is essential to a unified design. Let the color, texture, or pattern relationships of the fabrics used from room to room produce the desired effects. You will see that combining and coordinating fabrics for your home represents one of the greatest challenges in design. But it is an enjoyable, exciting experience and can be highly successful when you make your selections based on carefully conceived plans.


## Student Learning Objectives

When you complete Unit Seventeen, you should be able to do the following:

- Identify three interior uses for fabrics. List and explain the characteristics essential to fabrics selected for each use.

- Given a solid-colored upholstery fabric, select compatible fabric textures for the window treatment and for a second upholstered piece of furniture for one room.

- Applying guidelines for mixing compatible patterns, select a fabric with a print design and describe in detail three other patterns that could be used individually with the identified fabric.

- Using established criteria, develop a complete color and fabric plan for a traditional dining room.

- Discuss how fabrics can be used in a room to solve the following design problems: poor furniture balance, no established theme or mood, lack of harmony or unity in existing pieces.

### Learning Supplement

An interesting way to incorporate another pattern into a room's design is through the use of a "contrast welt." A *welt* is a strip of material sewn between upholstery seams to give a finished appearance. This piece of material usually has cording running through it and can be made of matching or contrasting fabric. When you visit a model home or a retail showroom, notice how contrast welting can be used to pick up certain colors in the design scheme or to enhance patterns used throughout the room.

After you have studied the available fabrics and narrowed your selections to a few, you may request loan samples of those and make the final decision in your own home. Because lighting and, of course, other fabrics in a room play quite a role in the suitability of a fabric, a sample offers a good solution to your dilemma. The retail store might take a few days to order samples from the manufacturer, but the end result is worth the wait. Most retailers extend this service at no charge, but the exchange is made in good faith. The consumer must return the samples in good condition and in the time stated by the fabric retailer.

It is equally important to request a sample cutting from the current dyelot of your fabric, as the sample you see may differ subtly, and perhaps even greatly, from the most recent run of fabric. For example, velvet-like fabrics from different dyelots often vary considerably in hue, value, or intensity from the original or loan sample. When ordering your sample, reserve the number of yards you will need from that dyelot. This temporarily holds the amount of yardage you need, preventing the problems that come with matching your fabric to that from another dyelot.

### Key Terms and Concepts

Pattern

Texture

Formal fabric

Informal fabric

Traditional fabric

Contemporary fabric

Current dyelot

Loan sample

Reserve

**Learning Activities**

- Complete the assignment in your text on pages 165-66 with these changes: Follow the specified instructions, but complete plans for three rooms rather than seven. Select any three rooms, but develop well-planned color transitions.

- Name three qualities essential to satisfactory upholstery fabrics.

- Suggest a second pattern to be used in the same room with a bold floral print.

- Explain how you can create unity and/or harmony in a room through the use of fabric.

- Describe one way that fabric may be used to deemphasize furniture or windows.

- Select one patterned fabric. Describe the desired theme for a specific room, and select two additional fabrics to be used as upholstery or window treatments for the same room.

- List and describe three fabrics appropriate for use in a formal, traditional room. How do these fabrics create a traditional mood?

- Describe the color, texture, and pattern of two fabrics that would fit well in a contemporary room.

- Explain how fabrics may be used to create transitional flow throughout a home without creating monotony.

**Optional Activity**

- Complete the full assignment found on pages 165-66 of *Beginnings of Interior Environment.*

**Optional Readings**

Sulahria, Julie, and Diamond, Ruby. *Inside Design: Creating Your Environment.* San Francisco: Canfield Press, 1977. Pages 145–48. Brief but good comments on fabric selection and coordination.

Whiton, Sherrill. *Interior Design and Decoration.* Philadelphia: J. B. Lippincott, 1974. Pages 535–57. Excellent background on the historical development of textile design. Helpful to understanding how to select fabrics that express a specific era.

# THE INS AND OUTS

## 18

## OF WINDOWS

For More Than Air and Light

**Assignments for Unit Eighteen**

1. Read the Overview, Student Learning Objectives, and Learning Supplement for this unit.

2. Watch Television Program Eighteen, "The Ins and Outs of Windows."

3. Read pages 220-23 in Part 7 of *Beginnings of Interior Environment.*

4. Review pages 156-65 in your text.

5. Consider Key Terms and Concepts.

6. Complete the Learning Activities.

7. Review the Student Learning Objectives.

## Overview

Windows and their decorative covers or treatments are a versatile yet practical way to make your decorating statement. Windows provide natural light, ventilation, and a certain amount of relief from the monotony of an unbroken wall. But it is the type of treatment that controls light, air, and appeal. Window treatments accent or eliminate a view, help establish the theme or mood of a room, provide insulation, and even reproportion an opening of awkward size or placement.

The purpose and mechanical operation of a window must be carefully evaluated before selecting an appropriate window treatment. Generally, windows are classified as movable or fixed. Within these two categories are many shapes, styles, and methods of opening. Windows may swing in or out, slide up and down, move side to side, or not open at all.

Windows that are movable and provide light, views, and climate control are probably most familiar to us. Double-hung windows have two frames that slide up and down, and swinging casements are hinged at one side and may swing in or out. (So plan a window treatment and furniture arrangement that does not interfere with its operation.) Sliding casements move from side to side in horizontal sashes and are easier to decorate and insulate than swinging casements. Awning windows are rather wide, horizontal panes of glass that swing out, as do the smaller paneled jalousie windows. Both types are very difficult to seal tightly, but they do offer good ventilation control. Bay windows and bow windows consist of three or more windows set at angles that project from the house to form an alcove. The ranch-style window, or horizontal strip of windows, is set high on a wall and consists of either sliding or swinging casements.

Fixed windows supply only light and view and are not common in our homes. Dwellings with this type of window must rely on expensive, mechanical ventilation systems. Examples of fixed windows are: skylights (windows built into ceilings), clerestories (high, shallow windows), arched windows (with a series of curved panes at the top), and picture windows (those that have a large single pane of glass).

Usually those window treatments enhancing the architectural lines of the window are considered architectural or structural, and those treatments that soften or disguise the architecture are referred to as "soft." Either type may be constructed of textile or nontextile materials.

When you choose a fabric for a window treatment, be familiar with the fiber's qualities and the care it requires. Determine just how much natural light filters through your fabric, as it varies considerably from fabric to fabric.

Although there are no set rules for the choice of window treatment, the design and styling of the fabric should be in keeping with the mood or theme of the room and should of course be based on the principles of design. Traditional and many formal settings call for opaque, sometimes heavy, fabric with elaborate borders and trims. This type of theme can be enhanced with tie-back overdrapes and an underdrape of some type. A more casual or country setting may make use of the homespun, natural look, small florals, and geometrics to set the theme. The more contemporary or modern mood calls for plain colors and more streamlined treatments with texture as the main point of interest. Sometimes a particular treatment will create as many moods as there are fabric patterns and textures.

Arched Window

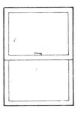

Double Hung

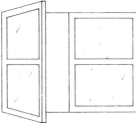

Swinging Casement

Swinging Casement
Variation

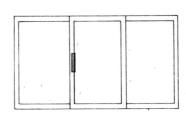

Sliding Casement

Awning

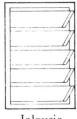

Jalousie

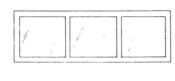

Ranch-Style Window

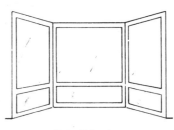

Bay Window

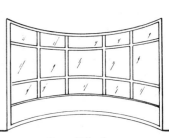

Bow Window

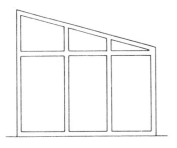

Window Wall Clerestory

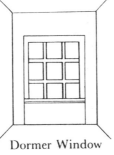

Dormer Window

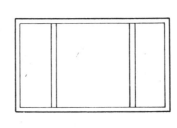

Picture Window

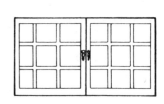

French Window

Curtains and draperies are two of the most common types of window treatments. Usually curtains are stationary and are made of sheer or light-weight fabrics. Draperies are made of heavier, sometimes opaque, fabric and may be either the stationary or the draw type. Draperies and curtains may be used alone or with shades, blinds, shutters, panels, and so forth. Generally speaking, curtains are more informal than draperies, but the texture, color, and pattern of the fabric influence greatly the ultimate look of the soft window treatment.

Draperies and curtains are constructed with a variety of headings. They may be shirred, pinch pleated, French pleated, or box pleated or made with tubular pleats ("cartridge construction").

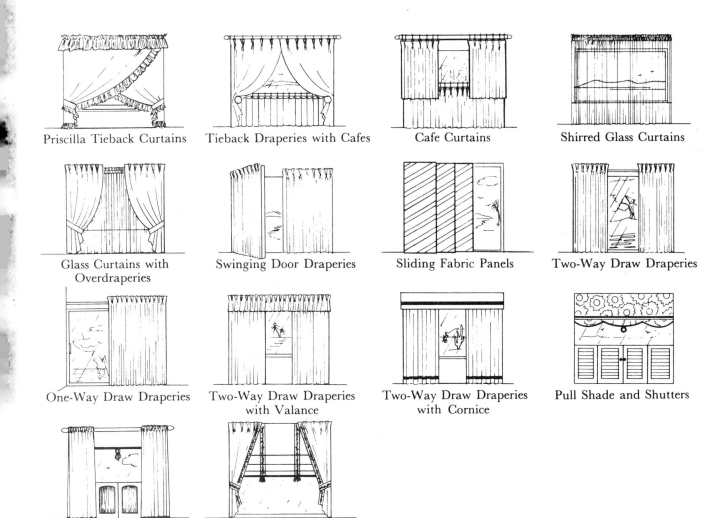

Priscilla Tieback Curtains    Tieback Draperies with Cafes    Cafe Curtains    Shirred Glass Curtains

Glass Curtains with Overdraperies    Swinging Door Draperies    Sliding Fabric Panels    Two-Way Draw Draperies

One-Way Draw Draperies    Two-Way Draw Draperies with Valance    Two-Way Draw Draperies with Cornice    Pull Shade and Shutters

Pull Shade with Side Draperies and Fabric-Centered Shutters    Roman Shade and Side Draperies

These headings may be covered with borders, such as valances, swags, cornices, or lambrequins. Borders add interest, uniqueness, and variety to an otherwise simple treatment and can be used to emphasize the mood of the room.

Today shades and blinds have assumed a much more important role in the decorative aspect of treating windows. They offer practical solutions for light control, insulation, and energy conservation. There are three basic types of shades: roller (simple yet versatile, suitable for decoration), Roman (folds into horizontal pleats when drawn), and Austrian (a formal elegant shade that folds in scallops or swags when drawn).

The standard Venetian style blind has taken on new dimensions today because of the variety of available slat widths and colors. These blinds can be made from metal, wood, split bamboo, fabric laminate, woven wood, or a combination of these. They may be hung horizontally or vertically and they can be custom made to your specifications.

Shutters may be used in traditional as well as very contemporary settings. They are available with fixed and movable louvers, fabric panels, fretwork inserts, or custom designs. They can be painted, covered with fabric, wallpapered, or trimmed to suit the decor. And they may be used in combination with almost any other window treatment.

Some windows may call for less treatment than do others, and if privacy is not an issue, partial treatment or no treatment at all may be appropriate. By all means capitalize on a sensational view.

If your budget allows, antique or custom-stained glass can be used, and it also provides a focal point in the room. Indoor plants may be arranged by a window to give partial coverage and create a dramatic effect when the sunlight filters through the lush greenery.

No matter how you choose to treat the various windows in your home, try to unify the exterior and interior; keep the theme or mood flowing throughout. Remember, too, all maintenance requirements and budget limitations.


**Student Learning Objectives**

When you complete Unit Eighteen, you should be able to do the following:

■ List at least five specific criteria to use when selecting window treatments, and explain how the application of each will help achieve functional and aesthetic goals.

■ Describe two appropriate window treatments for both traditional and contemporary room settings.

- Give one reason for selecting each of the following window treatments in preference to draperies or curtains: shutters, roller shades, Venetian blinds, a plant grouping.

- Identify three characteristics indicative of quality construction in draperies and curtains.

- Given window-treatment problems for a specific room, plan two window treatments that will correct the problems.

## Learning Supplement

Whether you decide to buy your curtains or draperies ready made, have them custom made, or make them yourself, it is essential that you measure your windows carefully.

Follow these basic rules to insure that your measurements are accurate:

a. Always take measurements with a steel tape measure or a carpenter's rule. Cloth tapes can stretch.

b. Write down all the measurements of each window as you take them. Recheck your measurements.

c. Measure every window—even if some appear to be the same size.

d. Measure the desired finished length of the window treatment. Floor-length curtains and draperies should barely clear the floor. For rooms with baseboard heat, choose a style and length that will not interfere with air flow.

e. Measure the width of the treatment you plan. If it has a return (the distance between the rod and the wall), add that measurement to the width.

Exterior window treatments are often overlooked as excellent remedies for heat control, ventilation problems, and light diffusion. They can provide this control without infringing on the interior plans of your home. In fact, exterior treatments can be used as the sole treatment of a window or to complement those used inside. Therefore, choose exterior window treatments with the same care you use for the interior.

The most commonly used exterior treatments are awnings, shutters, overhangs, grilles or fences, and louvers. Awnings made of weather-resistant fabrics or metal may be stationary or movable, allowing for easy adjustment. Today shutters are not as common as they once were, and they have evolved into fixed, decorative attachments. But when functional, shutters can provide insulation and also filter light. Overhanging roofs are popularly used in construction today for shade and for filtering light, and as shelter for outdoor living spaces. Grilles or fences placed close to a window can offer needed privacy as well as sun and wind control.

Louvers of wood, metal, or plastic can also be quite effective as sun shades and weather-protection devices.

It is not always easy to visualize how a window treatment will relate to the wall on which it will be placed, to adjoining walls, or to the entire room. A scale elevation drawing provides a good opportunity to see the general effect. Occasionally, you may want to include an adjoining wall to determine the impact of the treatment on the room as a whole. Just add your desired window treatment effect to the standard wall elevation. (See pages 259 and 282 of our text for additional examples as well as samples below.)

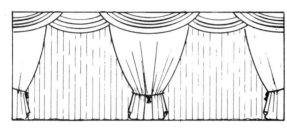

One Wall

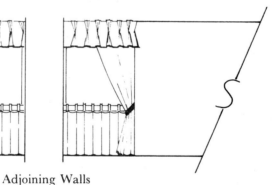

Adjoining Walls

**Key Terms and Concepts**

Curtain

Drapery

Casement fabric

Structural or architectural treatment

Soft treatment

Jalousie

Casement windows

Cornice

Valance

## Learning Activities

- Evaluate the window types of each room in your home. Consider the direction of exposure, and describe how the windows control ventilation, light, and heat.

- Design treatments for the following "problem" windows:
  a. Windows located at different heights on the same wall
  b. A pair of double-hung windows not centrally located on a wall
  c. A series of windows placed above an architectural detail such as a radiator or heating vent.

- Plan an exterior window treatment for one of the windows in your home. Explain why the treatment would be both functional and aesthetically pleasing.

## Optional Activity

- Using a particular window in your home, design a window treatment that incorporates both architectural and soft type treatments. Keeping in mind the theme of the room, list textures and patterns of all materials that would be used.

## Optional Readings

Faulkner, Ray, and Faulkner, Sarah. *Inside Today's Home.* New York: Holt, Rinehart and Winston, 1975. Pages 325–47. Excellent information. Extensive coverage of window types and functions, interior and exterior treatments, and types and functions of curtains and draperies.

*How to Make Your Windows Beautiful.* Michigan: Kirsch Company, 1976. Window treatment ideas. Hardware discussed and illustrated in detail.

Whiton, Sherrill. *Interior Design and Decoration.* Philadelphia: J. B. Lippincott, 1974. Pages 569–84. Terminology of draperies and curtains. Period styles. Types of uses of valances and cornices.

# WHAT TO MAKE

**19**

## OF A WALL

Make It Work with Paint and Wood

**Assignments for Unit Nineteen**

1. Read the Overview, Student Learning Objectives, and Learning Supplement for this unit.

2. Watch Television Program Nineteen, "What to Make of a Wall."

3. Read pages 201-20 in Part 7 of *Beginnings of Interior Environment*.

4. Consider Key Terms and Concepts.

5. Complete the Learning Activities.

6. Review the Student Learning Objectives.

## Overview

Because walls occupy more space than any other single element in a room, they must be considered an extremely important part of your overall design. Today's new materials, technology and popularity afford an unending variety of materials that add interest to walls.

There are several factors to consider before you decide on the wall covering or combination of wall coverings that will be used in a particular room. You should first determine the function of the room and the mood you want to establish. The scale of the walls can dictate the intensity of patterns you may choose as well as the value of the color. Consider, too, other furnishings within a room when selecting wall treatments. Furniture and wall-treatment choices should correspond in theme or mood. For instance, if your furnishings are traditional, you may want to choose wall treatments in patterns that are historical reproductions. However, if your furniture is sleek and modern, a brilliant wall graphic may be the appropriate selection.

Carefully planned wall treatments can emphasize or supplement the furnishings in a room. If you have a minimum of furnishings and accessories, a strong-patterned wall treatment can take the place of pictures or wallhangings, filling in around the limited furnishings. Conversely, walls can be an unobtrusive background for art work and furniture. Also, you may feel that your furniture arrangement would be complimented by making one wall a focal point and the others in the room more neutral. This is all possible with wisely selected wall treatments.

The first impulse of many people is to paint walls; paint is popular because it can be applied easily and quickly—and inexpensively—as compared with other wall treatments. Even though painted walls are usually less obtrusive in a room scheme, paint can also be used for dramatic graphic effects and in combination with other materials for added emphasis. But even with all of its assets, paint is not always the best choice. When you need additional insulation, accoustical or textural qualities, another type of wall covering would be a wiser choice.

The variety of available paints and colors can cause the consumer a great deal of confusion. Never hesitate to ask questions of reliable dealers. The type of paint you finally choose should be dependent upon the mood of the room, the use it will receive, and the areas surrounding the walls to be painted.

Almost all paints can be divided into three basic categories: solvent-thinned, water-thinned, and catalytic coatings. Solvent-thinned paints are used mainly for exterior surfaces. They dry slowly, have a strong smell, and must be thinned with turpentine or mineral spirits. Painting equipment must be cleaned with some type of solvent. If you do use this type of paint, make sure the room is well ventilated.

Water-thinned paints can be used on interior or exterior surfaces. They dry quickly, and tools may be cleaned with water. This type of paint is referred to as latex and may be a composition of rubber, acrylic, and vinyl. Also included in this category are emulsion paints that usually cover surfaces with one coat.

Catalytic paints, which are hardened by chemicals, provide the most durable finish. Although they may be used on most surfaces, they are not easy to apply. In addition, catalytic paints, including epoxy, urethane, or polyurethane, are expensive and emit irritating fumes.

Most paints are available in a variety of finishes. It is important to consider finish when you are selecting an appropriate paint. Finishes include flat, gloss, semigloss, eggshell, and textured.

Flat paint should be used on walls that will receive minimum wear. Flat paint is easy to apply, can be wiped clean, and does not reflect light.

Enamels come in gloss, semigloss, and eggshell finishes. They provide excellent wear and should be used on surfaces that will need frequent scrubbing such as doors and moldings. Eggshell enamels, the least glossy, have been used traditionally in kitchens and bathrooms, but may also be a good choice for hallways.

If you have rough or damaged surfaces to cover, textured paints could be the solution. These paints either have a "sand" finish or resemble adobe or stucco.

Keep in mind that no matter what type of paint you use, you should read the labels carefully and obtain all necessary information and equipment before you begin.

The use of wood in all types, shapes, and sizes for wall treatments is very popular because the rich look of wood adds to the aesthetic quality of any room. Depending on the tone, texture, and quality of the wood used, wood may simply and attractively set a mood of formality or informality.

A variety of sizes and shapes are available in precut and finished wood panels and squares. Wood may be installed alone or in combination with paint, wallpaper, or other wall coverings. Woods most commonly used are pine, walnut, redwood, birch, maple, and oak. If you desire more grain patterns and variation in tone, you might choose from teak, rosewood, or zebrawood. Wood is available in an endless variety of textures and prices. If the wood is well chosen, you can count on a lifetime of beauty and warmth with very little care.

Paint and wood, the two most versatile and popular wall treatments, can be an appropriate choice for any room. However, your wall-treatment selections, whether paint, wood, or any other, should be based on the interrelationship of established needs, total cost, and of course the design principles.

## Student Learning Objectives

When you complete Unit Nineteen, you should be able to do the following:

- List and explain how to apply at least five factors to be used when selecting wall treatments for a room.
- Applying color selection criteria, select for three walls a paint color compatible with the wallpaper you have chosen for the fourth wall within a room.
- Using at least two values of one hue, illustrate a paint color scheme for a room. Describe the specific uses of each color value, and explain the visual effect of the total plan.
- Discuss the general characteristics, uses, and visual effects of at least two types of wood paneling, and explain why the identified types would or would not be a good choice for a hard-use area.
- Plan and describe three "special-effect" wall treatments for three different rooms, using either paint or wood.

## Learning Supplement

When selecting paint colors, make certain they can be reproduced later. Record your choice by name and number, adding any other decorating information that later may prove useful. You might save paint chips, make your own samples, or save the stir stick from the paint can. Use these samples for coordinating or matching other decorating items as well as paint.

To understand the subtleties involved in color choices for walls, review Part Five, "Color Use and Misuse," in your text.

Note that paint generally dries somewhat lighter than when it is applied, so you should test custom-mixed colors before painting an entire room. Don't forget to check the color in both daylight and artificial light.

## Key Terms and Concepts

Graphic wall treatment

Solvent-thinned paint

Water-thinned paint

Catalytic paint

Flat finish

Semigloss

Gloss

Enamel

Eggshell finish

**Learning Activities**

■ Evaluate three rooms in your own home. To what extent does each wall treatment represent the mood you planned to create? If your room or rooms lack interest, choose a more compatible wall treatment that will enhance the overall scheme. Explain how wall treatments, furniture, and fabric styles work together to create a unified whole.

■ Using paint, wood, or combinations of these materials, plan and describe three "special-effect" wall treatments for three different rooms.

■ Explain how an appropriate choice of wood for a wall treatment can set the feeling of formality in a room.

**Optional Activity**

■ Create a file of at least ten interesting wall treatments that use paint, wood, or a combination of the two. Briefly describe the feeling or effect of each.

**Optional Readings**

Collins, Peggie Varney, and Collins, Shirley Wright. *Putting It All Together: A Consumer's Guide to Home Furnishing.* New York: Charles Scribner's Sons, 1977. Pages 65–66 and pages 69–78. Excellent information on wood as wall coverings. Complete, descriptive consumer information on paints and stains. Good shopping hints and measuring guides.

*Better Homes and Gardens Decorating Book,* 3rd edition. Des Moines: Meredith Corporation, 1975. Pages 154–61 and pages 170–75. Good sections on how to paint and how to install wood paneling.

# DRESS YOUR

## 20

## WALLS

### Consider Wallpaper or Fabric

**Assignments for Unit Twenty**

1. Read the Overview, Student Learning Objectives, and Learning Supplement for this unit.

2. Watch Television Program Twenty, "Dress Your Walls."

3. Read pages 201-16 in Part 7 of *Beginnings of Interior Environment*. Pay particular attention to pages 206-16 for this unit.

4. Consider Key Terms and Concepts.

5. Complete the Learning Activities.

6. Review the Student Learning Objectives.

## Overview

Decorating with wallpaper and fabric is not an innovation of the twentieth century. But the tremendous variety of patterns and uses for these is a remarkable evolution.

Before you decide what type of wall covering you should use and the extent to which it will be used, assess the particular area and situation. Wallpaper can hide some structural irregularities, but if the room or area is plagued by cracks, patches, or even holes. another material would serve better.

Pattern in wallpaper or fabric can disguise many of the architectural irregularities that some homes have such as jogs, soffits, and even exposed conduits. If you are trying to trick the eye and conceal problems, a paper with an all-over pattern and random design would do the job best. Keep in mind that the scale of a wall-covering pattern should relate to the size of the area in which it will be used. A very small pattern would become lost if used over a large expanse, and a bold, colorful pattern becomes even stronger when applied on the walls.

Think about the design in wall coverings in relation to the theme or mood you wish to establish. There is a wall covering to blend or contrast with any style of furnishing.

Vinyl- and fabric-backed coverings are most commonly used today. They can be easily stripped off walls, and some can even be reused. The variations in vinyl wall coverings are: vinyl protected, vinyl latex, coated fabric, and plastic foams. (See pages 209-10 in your text.)

Designs currently available in wallpaper can be classified as: damasks, toiles, florals, geometrics, scenics or murals, almost naturals, metallic foils, and flocks.

Damasks, which represent some of the oldest wall designs, are used most often in traditional room settings. Symmetrical fruits and flowers encased in curves are the usual motifs.

Toiles consist of stylized floral patterns or landscapes on a creamy background. They can be reproductions of eighteenth-century fabrics. These wall coverings fit well in traditional or period room settings.

Florals encompass a wide category. They may be found in almost every color, style, and scale and can be chosen to establish many moods or themes.

Geometrics consist of any design based on straight lines, circles, or any combination of these. They are appropriate in any room setting. For example, stripes work well in a traditional room, and any geometric style blends into an eclectic design. Also checks look quaint and provincial in early American settings, while bold, large graphics add interest in modern design.

Scenic or mural papers have one large design meant to cover an entire wall. They can make areas look larger or can give a *trompe l'oeil* (three-dimensional) effect.

Almost naturals include simulated grasscloths and materials that look like leather, tile, or brick. Many of these papers are so effective that they look almost like the real thing.

Metallic foils usually have a paper backing, a thin layer of foil, and then a printed or flocked pattern, depending on the style. These papers are extremely fragile and may be damaged easily in both application and use.

Flocks are made by an electrostatic process. Synthetic fibers are attached to a paper backing to form the pattern and texture. Even if the background and flock are the same color, the contrast in textures gives a two-color appearance.

Wallpaper can be relatively inexpensive or very costly depending on the design or pattern, the number of colors, and additions such as vinyl coating, flocking, fabric backing, and the like. Beyond the cost of materials, what you are paying for in expensive papers is the design and its exclusiveness. The most expensive wallpapers are the products of the latest fashion in this industry.

Notice the "run number" listed on a roll of wallpaper. Make sure that all the rolls you purchase of the same pattern have corresponding run numbers. There is usually quite a color variation from run to run.

If you want the special textures offered only by fabric, or want a wall to match a window treatment and no paper is available, fabric can be applied to your walls. There are five ways to apply fabric: shirring, masking tape, velcro, staples, and paste. Be aware, however, that fabric is usually more expensive than wallpaper.

If you do choose to use fabric on a wall and plan to use glue or paste, make sure your fabric is thick enough. The fabric should also be resistant to stain, mildew, fading, and shrinkage. Some fabrics can be sprayed for increased stain resistance after they are fixed to walls. After the fabric is on the wall, you will probably want to apply some type of molding or trim at the top, the bottom, and the seams for a finished look.


### Student Learning Objectives

When you complete Unit Twenty, you should be able to do the following:

- Evaluate two given wallpapers in relation to functional and aesthetic characteristics for a small bathroom.

- Select three compatible wallpapers for use in three adjoining rooms that can be seen simultaneously.

- Correctly identify three different wallpaper design categories. Suggest a room theme for each, and explain how the design would help to establish the identified theme.

- Describe at least two flexible wall coverings and explain functional and aesthetic characteristics of each.

## Learning Supplement

Before you purchase any wallpaper, you need to estimate the amount needed. Do not skimp. It is better to have too much than too little.

Usually there are 36 square feet in each single roll of wallpaper. However, because some waste occurs in cutting and fitting, you can depend on using only about 30 square feet. The linear footage will vary according to the width of the paper.

The linear-foot system does not allow much margin for error. The edge of a room is measured for the number of widths of paper needed (the wallpaper could be 18 to 36 inches wide, depending on your selection). This figure is multiplied by the height of the room (in feet).

The square-foot system is a much safer one but has about a 20 percent waste factor. Multiply the width of the wall by the height. Then deduct one-half single roll for each large opening such as a door or window.

When measuring according to either system, you must take the drop match into consideration. The drop match is the frequency of the design's repetition (the rate is usually listed on the back of the wall covering). According to the pattern, this may require doubling or tripling the amount of paper required. It not only increases the initial cost, but it may also require a more experienced hand to apply it.

Three inches of a drop match is usually lost in every length since there must be at least three inches left at the bottom for trimming and filling. The greater the distance between drop matches, the more paper is lost in the cut. For example, a 33 inch drop match works ideally on an 8-foot-high wall, because three repeats of the pattern (99 inches) will provide 96 inches of linear coverage plus 3 inches for trim.

Here are some points to consider when hanging wallpaper:

- Always properly prepare walls before applying any type of wall covering.

- Remove old wall coverings, and start with a clean wall.

- When working with delicate wall coverings such as foils, silks, or handprints, begin by hanging a special paper without color or design (called "blank stock") as a base to cover imperfections.

- If walls are painted with gloss or semigloss enamel, the surface must be sealed before applying paper. Sealer must be used on raw wood or unpainted plaster walls as well.

- If grease spots exist, seal them with clear shellac. Always use the type of adhesive indicated by your particular wallpaper.

If you decide to employ a professional paperhanger, get a bid for all work to be completed such as sanding, sealing, patching, blank stocking, and papering. You may want the option of preparing the walls yourself, and then have the professional do the actual hanging of the wallpaper. Be sure you have a sample of the paper to show the professional. He will give you an estimate for the number of rolls needed. (This is advisable, because if you do return any wallpaper, the supplier may charge a service fee. Furthermore, usually only full, uncut bolts are accepted.)

## Key Terms and Concepts

Damasks

Toiles

Geometrics

Scenics or murals

Metallic foils or mylars

Flocked wallpaper

Special characteristics: prepasted, pretrimmed, strippable, scrubbable

Vinyl-protected wallpaper

Bolt

Run number

Flexible wall coverings

Blank stock

## Learning Activities

- Describe at least one advantage and one disadvantage of both wallpaper and fabric.

- Select several samples of different types of wallpaper, and illustrate the coordination and compatibility of these papers for one particular room of your home.

- Select three different wallpapers or fabrics to be used in three adjoining rooms that can be seen simultaneously. Explain why these treatments would be compatible.

## Optional Activities

■ Add to your interior-design resource file at least ten illustrations of wallpapers or fabrics. List how these illustrations represent functional and aesthetic characteristics that you learned in this unit.

■ Evaluate three rooms in your own home, and determine appropriate treatments, using different categories of wallpaper or fabric.

## Optional Readings

*Better Homes and Gardens Decorating Book,* 3rd edition. Des Moines: Meredith Corporation, 1975. Pages 153–84. Comprehensive information on a variety of wall treatments and specific installation procedures. Nice selection of pictures that illustrate interesting uses and combinations of wall treatments.

Faulkner, Ray, and Faulkner, Sarah. *Inside Today's Home.* New York: Holt, Rinehart and Winston, 1975. Pages 296–314. Good information on all types of wall treatments. Excellent chart discussing the character, uses, advantages and disadvantages of various treatments.

Sulahria, Julie, and Diamond, Ruby. *Inside Design: Creating Your Environment.* San Francisco: Canfield Press, 1977. Pages 229–45. Good information on selecting various wall coverings.

# WALL TO WALL

## 21

## Varieties in Backgrounds

**Assignments for Unit Twenty-One**

1. Read the Overview, Student Learning Objectives, and Learning Supplement for this unit.

2. Watch Television Program Twenty-One, "Wall to Wall."

3. Review pages 201-16 in Part 7 of *Beginnings of Interior Environment.* Pay particular attention to pages 201-6.

4. Consider Key Terms and Concepts.

5. Complete the Learning Activities.

6. Review the Student Learning Objectives.

**Overview**

Even though paint, wood, wallpaper, and fabric are the more commonly used products for wall treatments, a wide variety of other materials can be used successfully to add interest to one or more walls in a room. Architectural glass in the form of mirrors is one of the most versatile of all wall treatments. Complete wall surfaces can be covered by mirrors, and the result is always a visual expansion in the size of the room. Even when architectural glass is used in small quantities in conjunction with other wall treatments such as wood or masonry, there is some visual expansion as well as increased design interest. The reflective qualities of mirrors can double the impact of a good feature such as a crystal chandelier or a garden view. Some points to consider before selecting mirrors for wall treatments are: (1) good-quality mirrors are relatively expensive, (2) they should be used only where the probability of breakage is minimal, (3) they must be meticulously clean to be attractive, and (4) they should be used where they will reflect desired images.

Carpeting for wall surfaces can be quite costly and is not used extensively, but it does provide excellent sound absorption qualities where needed. It also adds textural interest and can be used to create unique effects.

The use of plastics or other materials that imitate such natural products as brick or stone is a matter of personal preference. Generally, these imitation products are less expensive, relatively easy for the homeowner to install, and may require less maintenance than the original material. Although the purist frowns on using imitative materials, they can provide a very attractive, serviceable wall covering when they are of a high quality.

There are other less commonly used wall-treatment materials—cork, tree bark, and leather tiles, for example—and new products will continue to appear on the market. As you expand your awareness of all of the available products and learn interesting ways to use them in your designs, always keep in mind cost, installation procedures, and required maintenance.

This lesson concentrates on how to make a good selection for a wall treatment to be used in any room. Although only a few different types of treatments could be shown in the program, the suggested guidelines can be applied to the selection of any type of wall treatment. Also shown is how to create a compatible mix of two or more wall treatments for one room.

More than any other aspect of a room's design, walls as background areas serve to set the mood or theme. When subtle in color, texture, or pattern, they represent a supporting background for the other design components. When visually stimulating, because of intense colors, bold textures, reflective surfaces, and dramatic patterns, they command more attention and may even become a primary focal point in the room.

The most important point to keep in mind as you make your selections is that any wall treatment must be selected in relation to all other aspects of the room's total design. Briefly review Units Three, Four, and Five to insure successful results. Remember that all wall treatments should express the mood or theme and the degree of formality or informality indicated by the other design components. Although some variety should be introduced in the room, a harmonious relationship of colors, textures, and patterns is necessary. For example, coarse grasscloth would be an appropriate wall covering for many informal rooms, but in a formal setting a finer texture would be preferable.

Very interesting design effects may be achieved by using different wall treatments on adjacent walls or by combining two or more varieties on the same wall. Whether or not you choose to use more than one wall treatment will depend on the design effects you want, and on the size of the room. Combining wall treatments will usually decrease slightly the apparent size of the room. As discussed in Unit Eight ("Focus on Color"), this may be advantageous when you are attempting to visually change the dimensions of a room.

If you do choose to use more than one treatment in a room, one material should be visually dominant. The dominant one should be used where emphasis is desired.

Consider, too, the compatibility of wall treatments used in different rooms that can be seen simultaneously. Although the rooms may be distinctly different, such as a living room and a bedroom, the wall treatments should not be so opposite or competitive with one another as to eliminate good visual transition. For example, two large floral patterns seen simultaneously may appear confusing, but using a large floral pattern in one room and an appropriately selected geometric in the other could produce a very attractive combination.


**Student Learning Objectives**

When you complete Unit Twenty-One, you should be able to do the following:

■ Given three illustrations of wall treatments using brick, ceramic tile, and mirrors, analyze the functional and aesthetic characteristics of each.

■ Describe one aesthetically pleasing wall treatment that combines mirror panels or tiles with one other material commonly used for wall treatments. Give a practical interior location for this treatment.

- Identify at least three factors that should be considered when selecting a wall treatment for a room.
- Discuss the importance of planning wall treatments for one room in relation to treatments used in other rooms that may be viewed simultaneously.
- Using two different wall treatments in each room and applying selection criteria for compatible colors, textures, and patterns, develop wall-treatment plans for both an informal and a formal master bedroom.

## Learning Supplement

How do you determine the degree of formality or informality in wall-treatment products? Many of the same criteria you use for fabric selection and coordination can be applied (refer to Unit Seventeen). Generally the most formal wall treatments are those that have reflective surfaces, very fine textures, light value and lower intensity colors, or a traditional pattern. Informality is expressed by nonreflective qualities, coarse textures, darker or more intense colors, or patterns depicting an informal subject matter.

Certain wall-treatment products can be used well in either very formal or informal designs. Depending on the other components in the room, nonpatterned ceramic tiles may be compatible in either a formal or an informal setting. Oftentimes, one type of wall covering will express varying degrees of formality, depending on its color, texture, and pattern. For example, rough-textured stucco walls are more rustic in mood than are stucco walls that are smoothly finished.

## Key Terms and Concepts

Masonry

Architectural glass

Coordinating wall treatments

Ceramic tile

Imitative products

## Learning Activities

- Describe at least one advantage and one disadvantage of each of the following wall-treatment materials: brick, stone, ceramic tile, mirror, and carpeting.
- Using a mirror to cover one wall, select and describe an interesting, attractive treatment for other walls in the same room.
- Explain how to determine the formality or informality of a wall-treatment product.

- Using two different wall treatments in each room and applying selection criteria for compatible colors, textures, and patterns, develop wall-treatment plans for both an informal and a formal master bedroom.

- Select compatible wall treatments for two different rooms that would be viewed simultaneously. Explain why the treatments are compatible.

## Optional Activities

- Develop an organized file of at least fifteen different wall treatments that illustrate unique uses or combinations of various products.

- Using magazine pictures of furnished homes, locate two rooms that illustrate poor examples of wall-treatment selections. Explain why the selections are not good, and give an example that would improve the background areas for each room.

- Through advertisements, brochures, or retail outlets, discover several new wall-treatment products. Determine cost, maintenance requirements, installation procedures and possible uses in an overall design.

## Optional Readings

*Better Homes and Gardens Decorating Book,* 3rd edition. Des Moines: Meredith Corporation, 1975. Pages 153–84. Comprehensive information on a variety of wall treatments and specific installation procedures. Good selection of pictures that illustrate interesting uses and combinations of wall treatments.

Faulkner, Ray, and Faulkner, Sarah. *Inside Today's Home.* New York: Holt, Rinehart and Winston, 1975. Pages 296–314. Information on all types of wall treatments. Excellent chart that shows the character, uses, advantages, and disadvantages of various treatments.

Sulahria, Julie, and Diamond, Ruby. *Inside Design: Creating Your Environment.* San Francisco: Canfield Press, 1977. Pages 229–45. Good information pertaining to selecting various wall coverings.

# CASING THE JOINT

**22**

## Learn to Recognize Quality

**Assignments for Unit Twenty-Two**

1. Read the Overview, Student Learning Objectives, and Learning Supplement for this unit.

2. Watch Television Program Twenty-Two, "Casing the Joint."

3. Read pages 227–29 and pages 243–47 in Part 8 of *Beginnings of Interior Environment*.

4. Review Parts 3 and 4 of your text and relate the information specifically to case goods selection.

5. Consider Key Terms and Concepts.

6. Complete the Learning Activities.

7. Review the Student Learning Objectives.

## Overview

Almost every room in the home will contain some pieces of unupholstered furniture. Although the term *case goods* usually applies to unupholstered pieces that provide some type of storage, such as buffets, chests of drawers, and consoles, some references identify all unupholstered furniture as case goods. For our purposes throughout this unit the term will be used to refer to tables and unupholstered or partially upholstered chairs.

Wood has been and still remains the most popular material for the construction of case goods. Although well-designed quality pieces may also be made of materials such as plastic, metal, cardboard, glass, and parts of plants (rattan, wicker, and the like), this unit emphasizes the standard characteristics of quality wooden case goods. Generally the criteria for selecting wooden goods can be loosely applied when you select nonwooden pieces. In addition, Television Program Twenty-Two offers many suggestions to help you determine whether a piece constructed of various nonwooden materials is a quality case good or not.

The most effective way to evaluate the overall quality of case goods is to inspect visually and by touch the following components: the structural and applied design, the finish, the hardware, and the construction materials and techniques. The basic structural design and applied design, if used, should be evaluated with reference to the principles of design.

Keep in mind that quality case goods, ones that exhibit simpler lines and little or no applied design, are usually less expensive than similar pieces that have additional decorative details. Be cautious of wood furniture with an excessive amount of "carved effects" created by fixing pieces of simulated wood onto the basic structure. Although it is possible to construct a well-designed quality piece at a reasonable price this way, the ostentatious use of simulated products all too often ruins a basically good design, and it frequently hides inferior materials and construction techniques.

A beautiful finish on the piece is indicative of quality. Finishes are applied to wood furniture (1) to enhance the natural qualities of the wood, (2) to change its color, (3) to protect it from damage by heat, moisture, and alcohol, and (4) to add decorative effects such as distressing and antiquing. (To "distress" a piece, manufacturers purposely dent, burn, slash or scratch the surface to achieve an informal or rustic look.) The type of finish selected should be in accordance with your needs. For example, distressed pieces are excellent choices for high use areas because a few additional dents and scratches will usually blend quite well with the original finish. High-quality finishes have a mellow glow, or patina, developed by hand rubbing and polishing, and are free of irregularities such as bubbles, brush marks, or extensive buildup of the finish in the crevices.

The design of the hardware should be in keeping with the overall design characteristics of the piece. Naturally, decorative quality hardware adds more to the retail price than simply designed structural hardware. Well-made metal hardware is usually heavy and is attached securely through a panel with screws or bolts. Less noticeable hardware pieces like hinges should also be checked for quality and ease in functioning.

When you are ready to evaluate specific construction details, look for a label indicating the type of materials used. If the information is not easily located, ask the dealer for the catalog that gives an accurate description of the piece.

The term *solid wood* indicates that all exposed parts are constructed with whatever solid wood the manufacturer claims to have used, such as genuine solid walnut. Hardwoods such as mahogany and pecan resist dents and scratches and hold joints more securely than such softer woods as pine and fir. Many of the beautiful solid hardwoods are premium material and are therefore considerably more expensive than the softer woods. However, special detailed hand carving and other effects can only be accomplished with solid hardwoods. If materials have been used to *simulate* wood carving, federal law requires that they be identified as such.

One of the best ways to determine the quality of construction throughout a piece is to study one of the drawers. The drawers should glide smoothly and have a stop to prevent its being unintentionally pulled all the way out of place. Although drawer interiors are generally not stained to match the exterior, they should be well sanded and finished. The sides and backs should be made of wood rather than particle board, and the upper edges of the drawer should be rounded. Note that sections should be connected by either dovetail or tongue-and-groove joints. The better-quality case goods have dust partitions made of plywood or fiberboard between drawers.

In addition to basic drawer construction, evaluate all other parts for quality materials and workmanship. Other strong joining methods used in case goods include the mortise and tenon, the dado, and the double dowel. Although some of these joints are not easily distinguished from the less desirable butt joint, a reputable dealer should be able to provide information about the specific construction method used. The lower edges of all tables, chairs, and desks should be smoothly sanded and finished. Some type of corner block should be included for additional stability inside standard joinings of corner sections. By all means, check the overall stability of a case good by applying pressure on all the sides. Look out for a wobbly piece.

Depending on the specific case good, there could be additional criteria to consider. For example, check the finish and apron details of table leaves to make sure they match the basic piece.

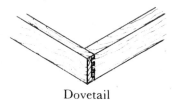

Dovetail

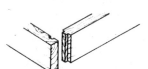

Tongue and Groove

Mortise and Tenon

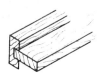

Dado Joint

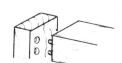

Double Doweling

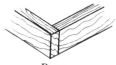

Butt

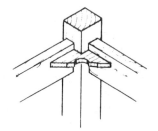

Corner Block

Such things as the presence of staples, excessive use of particle board, and poorly matched joinings filled in with glue or other material are signs of possible inferior quality in both materials and construction.

If you apply the suggestions found in this unit, you will have an excellent foundation upon which to judge the quality of case goods. In addition to your personal evaluation, the most important consideration for obtaining initial and long-term satisfaction with your case goods is to purchase from reputable dealers who take pride in their products and in their service to customers.

Reinforced Butt

## Student Learning Objectives

When you complete Unit Twenty-Two, you should be able to do the following:

- Define and explain the use of each of the following materials found in case good construction: hardwood, solid wood, veneer, and particle board.

- Identify the advantages and disadvantages of the following materials used in case goods construction: pine, chrome, molded plastic, clear glass.

- Analyze the information on a case-goods label in relation to the use, probable price range, and quality of the piece.

- Identify and evaluate specific parts of any wood drawer in relation to quality construction.

## Learning Supplement

*Cardboard furniture,* including pieces made of laminated fiberply, are reasonably priced and usually quite strong. Because of the construction technique—layers of corrugated cardboard laminated in alternate directions—these pieces are sturdy and can be unusually shaped. Also, cardboard absorbs sound and can have a suedelike surface. These qualities certainly make cardboard furniture an interesting alternative to wood and worthy of some consideration.

*Particle board* is made by combining wood flakes with a resin binding agent and pressing the mixture into sheets. Because it is less expensive than wood, particle board can be used for unexposed parts of furniture. This in turn will help keep the retail prices lower than if the same piece were constructed totally of wood. The exposed surfaces of the particle board may or may not have a hardwood veneer laminated to them.

*Simulated wood* includes several types of products. It may be a print of the desired wood imposed on another less expensive wood, or it could be a wood design printed on paper with the addition of a plastic surface coating and a plywood backing. Simulated wood carvings may be constructed of such things as rigid plastics and materials similar to particle board.

Reputable furniture retailers will stand behind their merchandise. However, if you do have a complaint, be sure to give the retailer the opportunity to offer satisfaction before you resort to other alternatives. If the problem stems from the retailer, perhaps the local Office of Consumer Affairs can provide assistance. But if the problem has to do with the manufacturer, and cannot be resolved through the retailer's communications with that manufacturer, you may find help by writing to FICAP (the Furniture Industry Consumer Advisory Panel) in High Point, North Carolina 27260. This organization will listen to consumer complaints and attempt to mediate a satisfactory settlement between the manufacturer and consumer.

**Key Terms and Concepts**

Case goods

Hardwood

Soft wood

Veneer

Simulated wood

Particle board

Quality-construction characteristics

Retail-cost factors

**Learning Activities**

- Identify four characteristics indicative of quality construction in furniture drawers.

- List one positive aesthetic or functional characteristic for each of the following materials used in furniture construction: chrome, fiberply, clear glass, hardwood veneer.

- Select one type of case-good item, and compare prices for this item at three very different types of stores. Identify the differences you discovered in construction materials, finishes, quality characteristics and exterior design details of the case goods.

- Ask four different people to identify specific consumer problems they have had when purchasing case goods. Discuss what each consumer might have done to avoid the problems or to resolve the situation.

- Identify three factors that will generally cause a case good to have a higher retail price.

- Define *veneer,* and explain its value to the consumer.

142

■ Describe how to best evaluate the quality of a finish used on case goods.

**Optional Activity**

■ Evaluate the three types of furniture-marketing methods presented in your text. Which method or methods appeal to you more, and why?

**Optional Readings**

Stepat-DeVan, Dorothy. *Introduction to Home Furnishings.* New York: The Macmillan Company, 1971. Pages 256–69. Excellent discussion of types of woods, construction details, and quality evaluation of case goods.

Sulahria, Julie, and Diamond, Ruby. *Inside Design: Creating Your Environment.* San Francisco: Canfield Press, 1977. Pages 288–93. Brief but excellent comments on evaluating quality in case goods.

Wingate, Isabel, Gillespie, Karen, and Milgrom, Betty. *Know Your Merchandise.* New York: McGraw-Hill Book Co., 1975. Pages 354–60. Good information on furniture and basic case-goods construction.

# FABRICS ON FRAMES

## 23

### Construction of Upholstered Furniture

**Assignments for Unit Twenty-Three**

1. Read the Overview, Student Learning Objectives, and Learning Supplement for this unit.

2. Watch Television Program Twenty-Three, "Fabrics on Frames."

3. Read page 230 in Part 8 of *Beginnings of Interior Environment*.

4. Consider Key Terms and Concepts.

5. Complete the Learning Activities.

6. Review the Student Learning Objectives.

## Overview

The old saying, "You can't judge a book by its cover," certainly applies when shopping for and selecting upholstered furniture. Because a great many of the quality check points are permanently hidden from view, you need to acquire a good working knowledge of terminology and construction methods before purchasing any piece of upholstered furniture.

Spend some time comparing types of construction and costs. After studying this unit, you should be able to identify quality construction techniques and ask appropriate questions.

Keep in mind that a lovely upholstery fabric cannot compensate for poor-quality construction. Quality upholstered furniture is a combination of fine fabric over excellent construction and materials. In fact, many interior designers make the suggestion that upholstered furniture should be selected from the inside out. Well-constructed upholstered furniture will give many years of durable, comfortable service. Poorly constructed furniture may look good when it is new, but within a few weeks or months, it may begin to sag or lump and become uncomfortable.

You will find that quality construction begins with the frame. All frames should be kiln-dried, good quality hardwood such as ash, alder, oak, birch, or maple. Each manufacturer will be governed by individual preferences and the availability of the wood. The only way you may be able to tell if a frame has been kiln dried is by the absence of warping and/or beads of sap. Frame joints should be a combination of glue and double doweling to withstand stress and strain. Corner blocks and screws should be used to reinforce all corners. Tightly woven bands of jute or strong webbing are interlaced and securely attached to the frame. (An excellent construction is produced by webbing that is closely interlaced and preferably doubled.) Heavy cotton material stretched across the chair bottom, back or sides, and held tautly in place with tiny springs, can be used instead of webbing. Sometimes steel or wooden slats are used in place of webbing or heavy cotton and springs, but they do not have the necessary elasticity for real comfort.

Highly tempered, enameled steel springs should be anchored to the webbing or stretched cotton. Twelve springs per seat is the best, and eight is the minimum. In better-quality furniture, the springs are tied to each other and to the frame in eight places with heavy hemp or flax twine to keep the springs in place and prevent sagging. Each spring is tied at right angles in two directions and diagonally, resulting in eight knots on each spring. Thus the phrase "hand tied eight ways" has come to denote fine-quality construction. Try to determine if the coil springs have been placed close together (not so close as to rub against one another) so that they produce a resilient, comfortable seat called "spring-edge seat." You can check this by touch or ask the retail salesperson.

There are other types of springs used in moderately priced furniture. Sagless springs are flat wavy lines of high-grade steel that look like grillwork. They are attached to the top of the frame and produce a "rigid-edge seat."

The difference between these two types of spring construction is cost and comfort. The sagless spring is less expensive than the coil spring, but the rigid-edge seat produced is not as comfortable as the soft, spring-edge seat. Although both types of construction may be durable if quality materials and techniques are used, you have to determine if the additional comfort warrants the additional cost.

The next construction step is to cover the springs with burlap. On the front edge of the seat a special reinforcement of rolled burlap is added. This gives the frame a soft edge and keeps the filling layer from working away from the edges.

Construction Examples

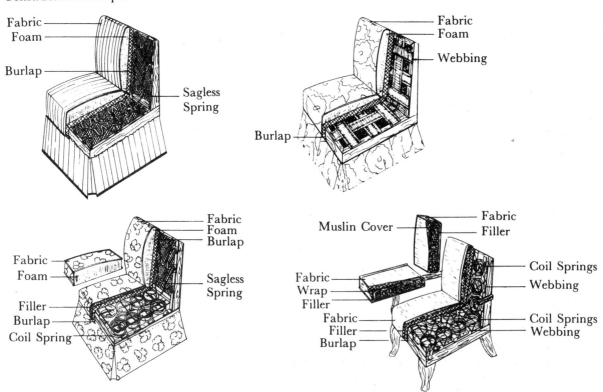

Adapted from an illustration by Philip F. Farrell, Jr. from PUTTING IT ALL TOGETHER by Peggie Varney Collins and Shirley Wright Collins. Copyright © 1977 Peggie Varney Collins and Shirley Wright Collins. Reprinted by permission of Charles Scribner's Sons.

Next, a layer of filling is placed over the burlap. Some fillers used are: kapok, sisal, cotton, goose down and feathers, or rubberized hair. Foam rubber has also become very popular in medium- to high-priced furniture. Synthetic fibers, sometimes a muslin cover, and finally the upholstery fabric blanket the filler. Even though the muslin cover relieves the extreme stress placed on the upholstery fabric, some manufacturers cut costs by eliminating the muslin.

As you will recall, suitable upholstery fabrics were discussed in Unit Seventeen. Make sure that the outer fabric is firm but not too tight. Stretched fabric will eventually lose its stability and sag out of shape. Whatever upholstery fabric has been selected, it should be used on all exposed parts and on the seat under any loose cushions. If less-expensive fabric is used on this underseat, it should not be exposed, even when people sit down and the cushions move slightly.

Any fabric may be used to cover upholstered furniture, but a tighter weave and a stronger yarn will be more durable. Be sure to check hang tags for fabric content, finishes applied, and care needed. If this information is not available, ask a salesperson.

It is almost impossible for a concerned consumer to physically check the construction quality, type of spring, and the like on a finished upholstered piece. Therefore, you should ask the retailer pertinent questions or ask to see a "spec sheet" listing the fine points of materials and construction techniques.

By following the guidelines presented in this unit, you should be able to buy upholstered furniture that will virtually last a lifetime. But in your search for quality, do not compromise on comfort. Sit on the chair or sofa for an extended time if possible. Notice the angle of the back, the depth and height of the seat, the height of the arms, and the firmness of the cushions. Unless the upholstered piece is comfortable as well as serviceable, you will find yourself hoping it can soon be replaced.

## Student Learning Objectives

When you complete Unit Twenty-Three, you should be able to do the following:

- List one advantage and one disadvantage of each of three common filling materials.

- Discuss the basic interior components of an upholstered chair having loose seat and back cushions, and explain how a consumer might evaluate these in relation to use and cost.

- Using a sofa upholstered in print fabric, evaluate the exterior according to design principles, quality characteristics, and possible price range.

- Demonstrate and explain how to evaluate upholstered furniture for comfort characteristics.

- Discuss at least three factors to analyze when determining whether or not to reupholster a used sofa.

- Outline a plan that, if followed when selecting upholstered furniture, would help insure long-term functional and aesthetic satisfaction.

**Learning Supplement**

Some additional points to consider when purchasing upholstered furniture are:

- All fabric seams should be straight and inconspicuous.

- If the upholstery fabric has a pattern, it should be matched at the seams. Loose cushions should form a pattern match with the rest of the sofa or chair.

- Consider any family allergies before selecting a fabric and filling. Check hang tags.

- If extra fabric is desired for matching draperies or bedspreads, be sure to order it at the same time you order the furniture. This insures that the dyelots will be the same.

- Don't overlook the practicality of chair arm protectors tailored from the upholstery fabric.

- If trims are used, check to see that they are neatly and appropriately applied.

Fillers or cushioning materials vary according to price range and should be evaluated as to the comfort, intended use, and expected wearability. Listed below are several types of fillers and the characteristics of each.

*Goose Feathers or Goose Down and Feathers*

- Found in expensive upholstered pieces only. May be specified for an additional charge.

- Considered luxurious and soft

- Can cause allergic reactions

- May deteriorate after several years

*Latex Foam Rubber*

- Used in moderate to expensive furniture

- Resilient, durable, comfortable

- Should be in solid sections for best quality—not bonded pieces

- May deteriorate

- Not mildew resistant

*Polyurethane Foam*

- Used in moderate to expensive furniture
- Does not absorb moisture
- Resistant to solvents, mildew, insects, and acids from perspiration
- Flame resistant

*Kapok and Sisal*

- Found in poor-quality furniture
- Infrequently used

*Hair*

- Found in some moderately priced furniture
- Resilient
- Can cause allergic reactions
- Possible odors from moisture (rubberized hair eliminates the possibility of odors)

## Key Terms and Concepts

Webbing

Frame

Jute

Flax

Hemp

"Spec sheet"

Coil springs

Tempered springs

"Hand tied eight ways"

Spring-edge seat

Sagless spring

Rigid-edge seat

Soft edge

## Learning Activities

- Discuss construction of an upholstered chair that has loose seat and back cushions. How can you determine quality in this piece?

- Describe one advantage and one disadvantage of each of the following cushioning materials: foam rubber, feathers or down, kapok, hair.

- Identify three factors that will generally cause an upholstered piece to have a higher retail price.

- Compare the cost of a muslin-covered upholstered piece with a comparable one that lacks the muslin cover. Remember that muslin covers the filling before the upholstery fabric is added. Was this attempt to reduce manufacturing costs passed on to the consumer?

- Why is a "spec sheet" important to the consumer? How much evaluation can be done without one?

## Optional Activities

- Visit a furniture store. Ask the salesperson if you may see a cross section of the upholstery method used in one of the sofas in their showroom. Evaluate the quality of construction using the guidelines given in this unit.

- At this same store, examine several chairs and determine the difference between chairs with coil-spring construction and those with sagless-spring construction. Try to feel the difference between coil-spring construction and sagless-spring construction. Note any price differences.

## Optional Readings

Collins, Peggie Varney, and Collins, Shirley Wright. *Putting It All Together: A Consumer's Guide to Home Furnishings.* New York: Charles Scribner's Sons, 1977. Pages 117–27. Comprehensive consumer information. Excellent graphics of construction. Listing of filling materials.

Sulahria, Julie, and Diamond, Ruby. *Inside Design: Creating Your Environment.* San Francisco: Canfield Press, 1977. Pages 293–99. Excellent check points to look for when shopping for upholstered furniture. Discusses buying furniture and having it upholstered with the customer's own material.

# FURNITURE

## 24

# MIX AND MATCH

A Look at Eclectic Design

**Assignments for Unit Twenty-Four**

1. Read the Overview, Student Learning Objectives, and Learning Supplement for this unit.

2. Watch Television Program Twenty-Four, "Furniture Mix and Match."

3. Read pages 227–51 in Part 8 of *Beginnings of Interior Environment*.

4. Consider Key Terms and Concepts.

5. Complete the Learning Activities.

6. Review the Student Learning Objectives.

## Overview

Mixing and matching various compatible furniture styles that enhance the mood or theme in a room can be one of the most challenging tasks in interior design. Throughout various periods of time, fashion dictated that rooms be planned around one distinct furniture style, such as American Colonial. Naturally this concept represents a very easy method for achieving a harmonious look among the furniture pieces. Today, however, most people have acquired an appreciation for the more unique, interesting effects created by an eclectic plan, one that incorporates a mixture of several furniture styles in a complementary scheme.

Eclectic designing provides not only an interesting and attractive room but also the possibility of using your furniture pieces with those of differing styles that you may want to add in the future. Also, you have the opportunity to collect several special pieces over a period of years and to see them blend well into an established scheme. And one of the best advantages of learning to mix a variety of furniture styles successfully is that the rooms will be highly individual and personalized.

Although the textbook and the television program provide a number of guidelines and helpful ideas on how to coordinate furniture styles, keep in mind that this aspect of designing is particularly subject to your personal preferences. For example, you may prefer a structured, organized environment created by more matching than mixing of the various design components. Or perhaps you enjoy the additional spark created by including a totally out-of-character piece in an otherwise unified setting.

Generally, however, a good approach to an eclectic scheme is to apply the guidelines presented in this lesson and in your additional resources. Although it is not essential to learn all the design characteristics of specific furniture styles, you will find it helpful to understand and communicate about furniture if you are aware of the main differences between the traditional, provincial, contemporary, and modern styles.

Although the program presents only one interior designer's opinions on how to develop attractive eclectic rooms, the concepts presented provide an excellent foundation upon which to add your own and others' opinions. The room settings shown express a certain degree of formality, but the same criteria can be applied to the development of an eclectic blend for the most rustic setting imaginable.

When you view the program, observe not only the attention given to specific furniture pieces, but also the importance assigned to compatibility among all components within the room. For example, the colors, patterns, and textures selected for fabrics, background surfaces, and accessories play a vital role in the achievement of a successful blend in furniture. But that is not all.

Even though these components may be compatible, if the actual furniture pieces are incongruent, a successful blend has not been created. The achievement of a well-designed eclectic room is highly dependent on your ability to select and coordinate *all* the components within the room so that the total composition expresses unity.

**Student Learning Objectives**

When you complete Unit Twenty-Four, you should be able to do the following:

- Correctly define the following terms as they relate to furniture selection: suite, collection, traditional, provincial, contemporary, eclectic.

- Select an illustration of eclectic interior design, and analyze whether or not the furniture pieces represent good coordination.

- Identify at least three characteristics of the formal traditional style in furniture.

- Discuss the appearance of two finished wood samples, and describe one good and one poor selection for a compatible wood mix with each.

**Learning Supplement**

The ability to correctly identify basic pieces can be helpful when you communicate your furniture needs and preferences to sales personnel. The furniture identification charts on pages 248–49 of your textbook provide good illustrations of some of the pieces you may select. Although the illustrations depict specific furniture styles, the terminology suits similar pieces that express a different style. For example, the side chair illustrated could be made with straight, classical Louis XVI lines or the ornate qualities characteristic of the Victorian style.

If you take the time to become knowledgeable about specific furniture styles, you will experience increased pleasure and satisfaction when you select furniture and develop your interior plans. Libraries, manufacturers' catalogs, and retail stores are excellent resources for obtaining information related to furniture styles.

Here are some guidelines to keep in mind when you approach a variety of styles:

- Determine the degree of formality desired in the room. Evaluate each of the pieces of furniture you have, or will be adding, according to this mood.

- Select furnishing components for the room—such as colors, textures, and patterns for the background areas, furniture, and accessories—that express a similar degree of formality.

- Consider refinishing or reupholstering your present furniture pieces to make them more compatible with the mood you are attempting to achieve.

- Use large, dominant, or highly decorative pieces as focal points. Employ less emphatic pieces and subordinate background areas in close relationship to the focal points.

- Use transitional pieces that express the same degree of formality to help pull together a variety of distinct styles.

- Consider using a tripod or a grouping of three various items, such as three different wood colors or upholstery fabrics. Even though these pieces need to have a relationship with one another, they will provide some variety within the room.

Rather than studying all the various furniture styles simultaneously, you might find it easier to study the styles of one particular country in the sequence of their development.

## Key Terms and Concepts

Traditional style

Provincial style

Contemporary style

Transitional style

Modern style

Mediterranean style

Formal room design

Country room design

Eclectic design

Tripod

## Learning Activities

- Create a furniture plan for a room in which you use a formal traditional chair and at least three additional compatible upholstered and unupholstered pieces. Discuss why each piece is a good design for coordinating with the formal traditional style.

- Discuss five guidelines that are helpful to achieving a well-designed, eclectic room setting.

- Describe the differences between a suite, a furniture group, and a furniture collection.

- Explain at least five possible differences between formal and informal room settings.

- Discuss and define transitional furniture pieces.

**Optional Activities**

- Complete the assignment on page 247 of *Beginnings of Interior Environment*.

- Select one specific furniture style that you find appealing, such as Queen Anne, Country French, or Modern. Complete an in-depth study of this style by using printed resources, manufacturers' brochures, and retail displays.

**Optional Readings**

*Better Homes and Gardens Decorating Book*. 3rd Edition. Des Moines: Meredith Corporation, 1975. Pages 73–88. Good descriptions of furniture style categories. Excellent chart that suggests how to coordinate various components within a room planned around a specific furniture style.

Whiton, Sherrill. *Interior Design and Decoration*. Philadelphia: J. B. Lippincott Company, 1974. Pages 2–415. Excellent in-depth coverage of furniture design, including history and style information from antiquity through contemporary periods.

# NOOKS AND CRANNIES

## 25

## CRANNIES

Planning Special-Purpose Areas

**Assignments for Unit Twenty-Five**

1. Read the Overview, Student Learning Objectives, and Learning Supplement for this unit.

2. Watch Television Progran Twenty-Five, "Nooks and Crannies."

3. Consider Key Terms and Concepts.

4. Complete the Learning Activities.

5. Review the Student Learning Objectives.

## Overview

Each room in a home has a traditional function. But, depending on how you plan and organize available space, any such room can serve other specialized and unique needs of your family. For example, a family room that has been traditionally planned for television viewing, reading, and conversation can be customized to include storage and facilities for viewing family movies, a home/office study center, or even artistic pursuits. Bedrooms provide areas for sleeping, dressing, and possibly for reading or study, but they too can be planned to meet special hobby needs such as model building and collecting.

Well-planned special-purpose areas and rooms obviously increase the usefulness of the home, but they can also enhance aesthetic qualities and psychological satisfactions. Providing space and adequate storage for all activities decreases the cluttered appearance of a home and relieves the frustrations that develop when we live in poorly planned environments. Special-purpose areas and rooms encourage family members to participate in activities that they might otherwise ignore. Also, built-in work and storage units can be planned to improve the appearance of less-than-perfect room features, such as an awkwardly located fireplace or window.

Usually, because of limited space, special-purpose areas are incorporated into a room that also serves other needs. However, when space is available, and your life-style dictates, you may decide to devote an entire room to a specialized activity. A sewing room and a photographer's darkroom are good examples.

Planning for special-purpose areas should take place as you develop all the other aspects of the room's design. Make a one-fourth-inch scale, two-dimensional drawing of the area you wish to customize, and include freestanding and built-in furniture as well as the interior spaces of the storage units. The drawings will help you determine if your special needs will be satisfied and how these spaces, when furnished, will relate to the other design components within the same room. (Review Units Six and Twelve in this stage of planning.)

Because special-purpose areas almost always require storage—provided by separate furniture pieces, custom built-ins, or a combination of these—this program concentrates on efficient storage planning to satisfy a variety of needs. Although the examples of special-purpose areas presented in the program include kitchens, home office units, and sewing centers, the same careful thought and planning should be used in designing any special-purpose area. As you view the program, try to determine how you could incorporate some of the ideas and suggestions to improve existing specialized areas or develop new ones in your home.

If you do decide to use the services of a cabinet maker either to build new units or to customize existing furniture pieces or cabinets, it is essential that you understand the importance of good communication and assignment of responsibilities at the onset of the project. Each person involved should agree upon exactly what the design entails, what materials are to be used, how much the job will cost, how the work is to be financed, and what the quality of the finished product should be.

A variety of services may or may not be provided by the builder, such as developing plan drawings for approval, purchasing all the materials, and completing the finishing details of the piece. If you want to decrease the overall cost of the job, you might like to finish some of the work yourself or buy the materials on sale.

## Student Learning Objectives

When you complete Unit Twenty-Five, you should be able to do the following:

- Discuss the importance of planning for special-purpose areas and/or rooms so that personal needs are met.

- Determine the steps in planning for the developing of a special-purpose area or room that satisfies functional and aesthetic needs.

- Given a list of needs and available space, complete an appropriate elevation and interior scale drawing for built-in storage.

- Determine the functional needs for an existing closet, cupboard, or drawer, and discuss a plan for customizing this area to satisfy needs.

- Recognize the importance of good communication and assignment of responsibilities when selecting a cabinet maker.

## Learning Supplement

A difficult decision that needs to be made when planning specialized spaces is whether or not to use individual furniture pieces or custom built-in units. Here are some questions to consider when making your decision:

- Do you have a mobile life style? If so, you may need freestanding or wall-mounted units that are easily moved and adaptable to new environments.

- Are there ready-made pieces that satisfy your requirements? Be sure to check for appropriate size, quality, special finishes, and custom details.

- What is the cost difference between ready-made pieces and custom-built units?

162

- Would individual pieces or one custom unit create the most pleasing effect? You might evaluate the possibility of using specially built modular pieces that, when used together, give the illusion of one custom-built unit.

- Would the location and type of built-in unit enhance or detract from the resale value of the home?

## Key Terms and Concepts

Special-purpose areas or rooms

Customized storage

Modular units

## Learning Activities

- List storage needs to be satisfied by an existing closet, cupboard, or drawer. Develop a two-dimensional, one-fourth-inch scale drawing of the interior of this space as customized to meet the established needs.

- Using Living Room Plan One in the Student Packet, develop a furniture arrangement plan with built-in or wall-mounted units that satisfy the following traditional and special-purpose functions: conversation grouping and informal entertainment, reading facilities with bookshelves, and a home office/study center.

- Define *special-purpose area or room.*

- Name three factors to consider when determining whether to use individual furniture pieces or a custom-built unit to satisfy special-purpose needs.

- Identify one special-purpose need you have for your home. Discuss how planning to satisfy this need could improve the functional, aesthetic, and psychological qualities of your living environment.

## Optional Activity

- Using the special-purpose need identified for your home in the Learning Activities, develop a plan for part of or one of your existing rooms that incorporates these special-purpose functions with other requirements for the same room.

## Optional Readings

*Better Homes and Gardens Decorating Book*, 3rd edition. Des Moines: Meredith Corporation, 1975. Pages 309–44. Excellent chapter on how to plan and incorporate storage into various rooms.

Faulkner, Ray, and Faulkner, Sarah. *Inside Today's Home.* New York: Holt, Rinehart and Winston, 1975. Pages 30–85. Includes information on planning for a variety of special-purpose needs throughout a home.

St. Marie, Satenig S. *Homes Are for People*. New York: John Wiley and Sons, Inc., 1973. Pages 185–201. Good discussion of guidelines for planning storage.

# A ROOM

## CHECK

**26**

Producing a Complete Plan

**Assignments for Unit Twenty-Six**

1. Read the Overview, Student Learning Objectives, and Learning Supplement for this unit.

2. Watch Television Program 26, "A Room Check."

3. Read pages 287-311 in Part 10 of *Beginnings of Interior Environment.*

4. Consider Key Terms and Concepts.

5. Complete the Learning Activities.

6. Review the Student Learning Objectives.

## Overview

Thus far in this course you have learned how to develop specific plans for furniture arrangement, use of space, storage, lighting, fabric coordination, and so on. This lesson will help you understand how to apply what you have learned from each preceding lesson, and how to integrate these smaller plans into a functional, *complete* plan.

A complete plan not only includes the selection and placement of all design details, but also incorporates structural components such as plumbing, electrical facilities, and built-ins. In addition to satisfying your basic functional and aesthetic requirements, you should also include the special considerations unique to each family: such factors as budget limitations, maintenance requirements, and accommodations for physical limitations.

When you coordinate a complete plan, you will probably find it almost impossible to weigh all requirements against the same standard. For example, "givens" in an interior, such as structural materials, color of carpeting and flooring, or presently owned furnishings must be taken into consideration when planning, even if these existing features are not exactly your preference.

Also, having a room function at its peak efficiency (i.e., having it serve a variety of practical purposes) may mean having to settle for less-than-ideal aesthetic choices. However, by knowing how to use the design elements effectively, you can often create illusions that camouflage or correct these choices. Complete planning gives you the opportunity to identify your priorities, recognize and correct problems, and determine when trade-offs are necessary before you begin purchasing.

Every room needs a comprehensive plan. Rooms such as kitchens and bathrooms, which have well-defined functions and established fixtures and storage, may require less time to plan than other spaces. But even there the benefits to be derived from careful planning are significant.

Your textbook provides excellent information to consider when you are developing plans for specific rooms. Since it would be impossible for the text to include every problem unique to your situation, pay particular attention to the many different factors to consider when designing a variety of rooms.

As you view the television program for this unit, be aware of the processes involved in developing complete plans for the three situations shown. In each case, the individuals involved identified their specific functional needs as well as the desired aesthetic qualities for the rooms. Ideally, complete plans should have been developed for the multipurpose living room and kitchen/family room before any design changes were implemented. However, recognize the benefits of stopping to develop a complete plan even if you have already begun making some design changes without a predetermined plan.

The functional needs for each room received priority in the designing phase and were followed by the coordination of the various samples that satisfied stated personal preferences. Keep in mind as you view the plans and architectural renderings that you personally might have different requirements for the same rooms or desire another mood, color scheme, or furniture styles. The plans shown were developed to meet the needs of these specific individuals and as such represent only one of several ways to design each room.

Professionally prepared architectural renderings (perspective drawings that depict the architect's conception of a finished room), being expensive, are seldom part of a complete plan. They are presented in this program to help you visualize the rooms as they will appear when completely furnished. But learn to visualize a completed room. Generally, the ability to do this is a result of concentrated effort and continued practice.

Every time you have the opportunity, view samples and mentally picture them in use. Then, whenever possible, compare your mental images with actual room settings in which the particular samples were used.

## Student Learning Objectives

When you complete Unit Twenty-Six you should be able to do the following:

■ Given a specific hobby or function, discuss two possible room designs for accommodating the activities. Include such factors as space, lighting, furniture, plumbing, storage, and electrical outlets.

■ Design a room to be used for at least three different activities, satisfying space, storage, furniture, and maintenance requirements.

■ Discuss at least five specific problems related to interior or exterior spaces that can be solved with well-planned garage designs.

■ Discuss how visual and living space within a dwelling can be increased by well-designed outdoor living areas.

## Learning Supplement

When the interior of a home is designed, there are many possibilities for improving the total living environment through thoughtful planning of extended spaces. Such areas as garages, carports, balconies, patios, and outdoor spaces may seem to have little relationship to the design of the home's interior, but when these spaces are planned in relation to the inside areas, they can solve some problems in the interior.

For example, garages and carports can provide storage for some items normally stored within the interior, create space for certain hobbies, and yield areas for clean up. Outdoor areas can also be planned to provide a visual extension of interior spaces. They may increase the total living space by providing areas for outside dining, recreation, and entertainment.

To make the best use of extended spaces, you need to apply the same basic guidelines and planning steps as in the development of interior room plans. Careful attention should be given to such things as low maintenance, electrical outlets, lighting, storage, and plumbing. And remember, extended spaces should relate aesthetically to the interior of the home.

## Key Terms and Concepts

Complete plan

Multipurpose room

Extended spaces

Architectural rendering

## Learning Activities

- Explain the differences between a complete plan and an individual plan such as a furniture-arrangement plan, a lighting plan, or a fabric-coordination plan.

- Create an organized file of at least twenty good specific solutions for rooms that have problematic multipurpose areas. Explain how you could satisfactorily apply five of these solutions in your present environment.

- Identify four functions for a combination living/dining room using either "Living-Dining Room Two" or "Living-Dining Room Three" in the Student Packet. Develop a complete plan for the room, satisfying the specified functions.

- Define *extended spaces*.

- Discuss at least five specific ways your total living environment could be improved by thoughtful planning of extended spaces.

## Optional Activities

- Develop a complete plan for "Child's Bedroom Four" in the Student Packet. The functional needs for this room include sleeping, dressing area, clothing storage, toy storage, study/play area.

- Analyze any furnished room as to how successfully it incorporates all components into a complete plan. Suggest changes that would improve the complete plan.

**Optional Readings**

*Better Homes and Gardens Decorating Book,* 3rd edition. Des Moines: Meredith Corporation, 1975. Pages 249–328. Good, helpful information for developing complete plans for all rooms and areas within a home. Good chapter on apartment planning.

Faulkner, Ray, and Faulkner, Sarah. *Inside Today's Home.* New York: Holt, Rinehart and Winston, 1975. Pages 33–85 and pages 476–91. Good information and suggestions that are helpful in planning complete rooms and outdoor extended spaces.

St. Marie, Satenig S. *Homes Are for People.* New York: John Wiley and Sons, Inc., 1973. Pages 34–183. Excellent content applicable to complete room planning.

# THE PERSONAL STAMP

## 27

## STAMP

Accessories Are the Final Touch

**Assignments for Unit Twenty-Seven**

1. Read the Overview, Student Learning Objectives, and Learning Supplement for this unit.

2. Watch Television Program Twenty-Seven, "The Personal Stamp."

3. Read pages 307–11 in Part 10 and pages 324–31 in Part 11 of *Beginnings of Interior Environment.*

4. Consider Key Terms and Concepts.

5. Complete the Learning Activities.

6. Review the Student Learning Objectives.

# Overview

Accessorizing is the most intimate, personal part of interior design. However, it is important to think through exactly what finishing touches are needed. At this point, rules may tend to become secondary, and a deviation from the usual may be just the spark your home needs.

When selecting and arranging each accessory, you should keep in mind the elements and principles of design, as well as the interrelationship of shapes, colors, and textures. Accessory and furniture sizes should be in proportion to one another and to the room as a whole. Accessories can frequently complete the balance, provide emphasis, and establish rhythmic eye movement within a room.

Even though the compatibility of a piece with its environment is important, accessories should be selected because they please you and your family. Neither the style nor the motif of furniture and accessories must match, but they should be equally formal or informal. Again, there are very few established rules pertaining to the use of accessories, so it is necessary that you train your eye to see what constitutes a beautiful composition of accessories. One very prominent designer feels that the only way to tell what does or does not go together is to experiment with a variety of pieces.

Nothing adds more warmth and personality to a room than objects you cherish. Keep in mind that accessories should tell visitors about the character of the people living in the home. Personality and interests should be expressed. This not only sparks conversation, but brings enjoyment to the occupants when special treasures are on display for others to appreciate and admire.

A plain or sparsely furnished room begins to come alive when well-chosen accessories are added. When the major walls and furnishings lack color and warmth, accessories can easily remedy the situation. Also, accessories can be used to establish the major color scheme of a room.

Accessories may be categorized as either functional or decorative, and some may be described as both. Specific purpose items such as lamps, clocks, mirrors, books, pillows, ashtrays, vases, and tableware are considered functional. But with just a little imagination, such items can be made very appealing. Small functional items may be clustered for attention and then given an added punch for appeal. For example, ashtrays and lighters grouped with an antique humidor or pipe collection provide more visual excitement than if they were placed randomly about the room. The objects chosen for their beauty alone are decorative accessories. These can include: paintings, pottery, floral arrangements, plants, crafts, personal collections, and family photographs.

Choices for accessories are unlimited. Interesting and inexpensive ideas can be found everywhere and can be incorporated throughout your home. You may find some exciting ways to brighten your home when you combine salvaged "junk" with imagination. Don't forget to keep your eye open when viewing model homes, retail displays, or friends' homes—or when traveling. Perhaps the most exciting source of accessories is your own inventiveness and imagination.

Now that you realize the value of accessories, how and where do you begin? Generally a wall area provides opportunity for a dramatic impact. However, do not position wall or any other accessories without a total effect in mind. Although some individuals have the talent to create successful compositions without forethought, most find that a careful plan helps them implement their creative ideas and even helps them distract the eye from design problems within the room. When you plan wall accessories, keep in mind that opposite walls should have comparable visual weight and the room should appear balanced.

There are several ways to preplan a wall arrangement. You can use one-fourth-inch scaled templates of your accessories on a scaled wall elevation, or you can draw a full-scale plan on brown paper and tape it to the wall for examination. You can also use available floor space. Simply block out the size of the wall area on the floor with pieces of string and then actually work with your accessories in this space.

Surface accessories divide and soften the visual expanses found in most rooms. The number used in a room or area depends on personal taste, style of accessories, and the mood of the room. Not all people can live with "organized clutter" any more than others could live with streamlined emptiness. For example, it would be impractical for a family with small children to incorporate numerous surface accessories into the design of the home.

Start your plan by placing the most important surface accessories. Determine where functional pieces and dominant decorative pieces should be placed in relation to the less important ones. Keep in mind the following: Your composition should be attractive from every angle; odd numbers of accessories make a more interesting grouping than even numbers; and according to the golden mean, varying the heights of two or more pieces results in a pleasing effect. Also place surface accessories so that they do not interfere with wall decor.

Once you plan and place your accessories, do not feel that your work must be static. Simple rearrangements and variation of placement can produce a refreshing new look in your room.

**Student Learning Objectives**

When you complete Unit Twenty-Seven, you should be able to do the following:

- Give at least three reasons for using accessories in an interior.

- List at least five ways to obtain a variety of accessories and discuss how to determine where the accessories may be well used within a dwelling.

- Using both functional and decorative accessories, propose and discuss well-planned accessory groupings for each of two given surface areas.

- Given a furnished interior, analyze the selection and placement of functional and decorative accessories in relation to the principles of design.

**Learning Supplement**

Here are a few guidelines to follow when you select and use accessories:

- Develop a list of needed accessories and compare it with what you already have.

- Plants, paintings, and lamps draw the eyes into corners and make the room seem more spacious.

- Accessories are generally placed where people normally look, where you want people to look, and at eye level.

- Groupings should contain a variety of shapes for a more interesting composition.

- Work from a center hub when you place groupings, thereby keeping the viewer's eye contained.

- Space between items in a grouping should be limited to less than the dimension of the largest item in the grouping. However, the arrangement should not be crowded.

- Achieve three-dimensional variety on walls by using deep frames, plants, and the like.

- Be aware of the relationship of objects to their background and to one another.

- Wall accessories should be anchored by having beneath them a piece of furniture that has greater visual weight than do the accessories.

**Key Terms and Concepts**

Functional accessories

Decorative accessories

Surface accessories

Preplanning

## Learning Activities

- Recall the wall arrangement and surface areas you viewed in Television Program Twenty-Seven. Refer to Fig. 27.1 in this guide. Try to identify the important accessorizing guidelines pointed out by the designer and some she overlooked. How would you approach the same situation? What parts of the arrangement appeal to you? Why?

- Using the information found in this guide, your text, and the television program, analyze your present accessory plan or, if you do not have a plan, create one.

- Discuss how the accessories in your home reflect your personality and life-style. Could you strengthen this decorating statement? How?

## Optional Activities

- When you visit a friend's home, analyze his or her use of accessories. How do these accessories reflect personal taste, individual personality, or theme of the room? Do the accessories accurately "describe" your friend?

- Examine the accessories used within your own home. Determine how a regrouping of a wall arrangement or of a surface composition could bring about a refreshing change in the room.

- Take a closer look at the everyday items found in the kitchen. Try to incorporate several of these pieces in your accessory plan. As suggested in your text, try to utilize fresh fruits and vegetables in some type of arrangement.

- Books, plants, and fresh or dried flowers blend well with any accessory plan. As you visit a friend's home or a model home, determine how the use of these items produced a warm, inviting feeling, or how they could have been used to "humanize" a room.

## Optional Readings

*Better Homes and Gardens Decorating Book.* 3rd Edition. Des Moines: Meredith Corp., 1975. Pages 233–48. Outstanding chapter on how to choose, plan, and organize accessories. One section emphasizes working with collections.

Sulahria, Julie, and Diamond, Ruby. *Inside Design: Creating Your Environment.* San Francisco: Canfield Press, 1977. Pages 264–82. Discusses functional and decorative accessories.

Faulkner, Ray, and Faulkner, Sarah. *Inside Today's Home.* New
    York: Holt, Rinehart and Winston, 1975. Pages 422–48.
    Discusses functional and decorative accessories and the qualities
    they bring to an interior.

Figure 27.1. A re-creation of the picture wall seen in Program 27.

# PULLING IT ALL

## 28

## TOGETHER

Details Make the Difference

**Assignments for Unit Twenty-Eight**

1. Read the Overview, Student Learning Objectives, and Learning Supplement for this unit.

2. Watch Television Program Twenty-Eight, "Pulling It All Together."

3. Read pages 287-311 of Part 10 in *Beginnings of Interior Environment.*

4. Consider Key Terms and Concepts.

5. Complete the Learning Activities.

6. Review Student Learning Objectives.

**Overview**

In this lesson you will learn how to create a transitional flow throughout a home, and you will recognize the importance of considering and evaluating possible interior and exterior architectural changes during early planning phases. In addition, this unit suggests a sequential plan for actually implementing your design ideas.

Before you begin to put your designs into effect, it is a good idea to evaluate each room plan in terms of its relationship to others so that you can achieve transitional flow throughout your home. In a home characterized by "transitional flow," adjacent rooms have a significant design relationship, viewer's eyes travel smoothly from one room to another. When transitional flow is successfully executed, the home is aesthetically more attractive, the environment is psychologically more relaxing, and (because the total interior space has fewer visual divisions) the size of areas may even appear larger.

Repetition of a specific element or an idea is usually the most successful way to achieve transition. The most popular methods used are the repetition of a particular theme or mood, a floor covering, a furniture style, or a specific design element, such as a color, a type of texture, or a pattern motif. One or more of these methods may be used within one dwelling. However, open-plan areas should usually be aesthetically designed as one room: there should be a comfortable visual transition between adjacent rooms. Although each room is uniquely planned, all rooms within a home should appear to belong together.

Architectural changes and improvements involve any type of construction details that in some way alter the basic structure of the home. They include major changes such as room additions, the removal of interior walls, or the complete renovation of a room. Or the work can be less complicated—for example, the relocation of a door or the addition or removal of a window. Certain architectural improvements involve not only the basic structure but also changes in other details like plumbing or electricity. Therefore, because architectural changes might affect the remainder of the room's design, the need for them should be determined early in the designing stage.

In interior design we are basically concerned with the effects of architectural changes on the *interior* plans. But, it is also important to recognize the potential benefits of exterior alterations to the total design plan. For example, relocating the front door could provide a separate entry hall in the interior. Or minor changes in the exterior styling of the home may better integrate the exterior design with the interior.

Most interior architectural changes involve "opening up" or increasing space within a home, such as removing a wall or enlarging a room. However, a room plan may be improved by "closing off" space. For example, an open-plan living room-dining room may be divided to separate the areas, or a large, poorly arranged kitchen could be reorganized to create a space for informal entertainment as well as an area for meal preparation and service.

It may be difficult for you to determine when structural changes should and can be made in your own environment. If you feel that there are some changes that may be beneficial, it would be helpful for you to arrange a consultation with an architect or an interior designer who also specializes in architectural planning. Architectural changes are costly, so it is important to evaluate the potential benefits in relation to their cost.

**Student Learning Objectives**

When you complete Unit Twenty-Eight, you should be able to do the following:

- Discuss the importance of and suggest at least three ways to achieve visual and psychological transition throughout a dwelling.

- Describe three ways architectural changes can enhance an overall design plan.

- Appreciate a well thought out and correctly implemented plan for a complete dwelling.

- Arrange in sequential order a given list of steps to be included in the development of a total room.

**Learning Supplement**

Once you have developed a complete interior design plan, where do you begin to implement your creative ideas? Should you paint walls first or install new floor covering? Now you must think through a logical sequence to complete the work that is indicated in each segment in your overall design plan.

There is no standard sequential work plan that can be applied to every design. Although this unit suggests a sequence for work implementation, your specific design may require a slightly different one. The important point is that you think through everything involved within each design phase, identifying the work that should be completed before proceeding with the next stage.

Architectural changes, minor and major, usually represent the first step in the implementation of your designs. This phase should be followed by the construction of built-in structures such as storage units, bookshelves, and window seats. Any plumbing, electrical, or similar work is generally completed during one of these early stages.

Once the basic structural changes are made, usually the next step is the treatment of background areas—the application of wall and floor coverings. The sequence for completing background surfaces is dependent on the types of products used and the installation procedures. For example, many people find it easier to paint woodwork before installing wallpaper and carpeting but would prefer having hard-surfaced flooring installed prior to painting.

Window treatments, furniture placement, and accessorizing are the final stages. These may be implemented simultaneously or individually. Generally, the order is based on the functions of the room, personal preferences, and budget.

## Key Terms and Concepts

Transitional flow

Methods to achieve transitional flow

Architectural or structural changes

Sequential work plan

## Learning Activities

- Define *transitional flow.*

- Name two good methods that can be used to achieve transitional flow.

- Describe two architectural changes, and explain how each could improve the design of a room.

- Discuss how to establish a good sequential plan for design implementations.

- Explain two possible problems that could arise as a result of not using a sequential implementation plan for design work.

## Optional Activities

- Using your present living environment or another furnished home, evaluate the use of transitional flow. Identify specific things that could be done to improve it.

- Tour a newly constructed home, and see how many major or minor architectural changes you feel would improve the overall plan.

- Identify and apply one or two simple changes to revitalize one of your rooms. Evaluate the results, and determine if you achieved the desired effect.

# PENNY WISE

**29**

# WISE

Spend Time and Talent, Not Money

**Assignments for Unit Twenty-Nine**

1. Read the Overview, Student Learning Objectives, and Learning Supplement for this unit.

2. Watch Television Program Twenty-Nine, "Penny Wise."

3. Read pages 315–24 in Part 11 of *Beginnings of Interior Environment*.

4. Review pages 324–33 in your text.

5. Consider Key Terms and Concepts.

6. Complete the Learning Activities.

7. Review the Student Learning Objectives.

## Overview

Good decorating need not be expensive. With practice and a working knowledge of the design elements you can design an aesthetic and functional home, even on a limited budget. The key to unlocking the chains of a limited decorating budget is to use the basics learned from the previous lessons and to apply your own imagination and ingenuity. You can substitute time, talent, and energy for money, and be pleasantly surprised by the effects of a few wisely spent dollars. Not only is this way of interior designing extremely easy on the budget, it also can be fun and tremendously self-satisfying.

When you are working within a limited budget, evaluate what resources are available. For example, what are your own personal limitations regarding time and talent? Or what existing furnishings can you draw from and use after they have a simple face-lift? Then, make a list of proposed decorating projects and how to accomplish each one. This is a great time saver and a real help in planning your overall home design. Also, this list is a safe way to store ideas you may wish to try later.

Perhaps your designs indicate replacing original furniture or introducing some new pieces. Keep in mind that you should always purchase the best quality your budget will allow. You might want to explore what is available in unfinished furniture, molded-plastic furniture, and even corrugated cardboard or fiberply furniture. If you do select any furnishings in these categories, always refer to what you have learned concerning the design elements and color theory. You will be pleased by the many good design features in these collections and how well the pieces adapt to your other furnishings.

If you are interested in a big decorative change, do not ignore the versatility of color. A fresh coat of paint in a new color is probably one of the least expensive ways to take advantage of the impact of color. Bright, cheerful, inexpensive fabric can be used in various innovative ways to revitalize a worn interior. Accent pillows, tablecloths, cushions, valances, and curtains are just a few of the simple, relatively inexpensive, but interesting roles colorful fabric can play in your home's interior.

Accessories are an extremely important decorating component when your budget is limited. Sometimes just rearranging existing accessories will give a new and interesting look to a time-worn interior. You might dig into family treasures and collections and display your finds tastefully. House plants are moderately priced and have a unique way of adding warmth and character to a home. They may even fill in where furnishings may be sparse. Try grouping several sizes and varieties for more impact than an individual plant provides.

You should approach minimum-budget decorating with the realization that saving dollars usually means spending your time instead. To stretch the budget, it is usually necessary to invest much of your own time, energy, and talent in the projects you have chosen.

If you need something to stimulate your own creativeness, there are many varied and valuable sources of ideas available. Interior design and decorating books, periodicals, home-furnishing manufacturers' brochures, friends' homes, and model homes are all possible catalysts for your imagination. When you find an idea that particularly appeals to you, tackle the project confidently and enthusiastically. All that is really needed to succeed is imagination and a spirit of adventure. Throughout a decorating project, maintain a positive attitude, and you'll be amazed at what you can accomplish. Nevertheless, an important aspect of any project is to ask for advice when you need it.

Budget decorating is not just for those who are financially limited. Many people enjoy the challenge of using their talents and ingenuity to create a unique interior in their home. You should always remind yourself that good design has no price tag.

### Student Learning Objectives

When you complete Unit Twenty-Nine, you should be able to do the following:

- Explain the importance of at least six factors to apply when planning satisfactory minimum-budget interiors.

- Describe five specific creative ideas, using paint, fabric, furniture, or accessories, that could be successfully incorporated into minimum-budget interiors.

- Maintaining the general functional and aesthetic character of a given high-budget interior, design the major changes that could be made to reduce the total room costs.

- Using both minimum- and higher-cost furnishings, design an aesthetically pleasing interior for one room. Explain why the minimum- and higher-cost items are compatible with one another.

- Explain two simple, inexpensive changes that could be implemented to revitalize an existing interior.

### Learning Supplement

The desire to change the design of one's living environment varies with each person. Some individuals need relatively frequent changes; others remain satisfied with few, if any, changes over a period of years. Generally, when rooms are well-designed, there is less desire or need to make major changes. However, almost everyone feels the need to revitalize a room at some time or another.

Even when you are working with a limited budget, freshening an interior can be easy and fun. If you plan to keep most of the room's original decor intact, you can still repaint the walls in a different color or intensity, use slipcovers or reupholster worn pieces, add bright wallpaper to previously painted surfaces, refinish or paint one or two case goods, and add trims to draperies, tablecloths, and curtains. You are limited only by your imagination.

## Key Terms and Concepts

Minimum-budget designing

Molded-plastic furniture

Fiberply

Revitalize interiors

## Learning Activities

- Design an aesthetically pleasing interior for a family room that has in it both minimum- and higher-cost furnishings. Explain why the minimum- and higher-cost items are compatible. List at least four other ways to save money when implementing designs in this room.

- Complete the assignment in your textbook at the end of Part 11, pages 334–35.

- Using fabric as a method of revitalizing a room, determine a simple, inexpensive plan for freshening a well-used living room.

- Use a picture of a furnished room and describe two simple, inexpensive changes that could revitalize the plan.

## Optional Activities

- Develop an organized file of at least twenty different minimum-budget ideas that stress use of time, energy and creative talent rather than money. Consider how each idea might be adapted to your own home.

- Tour several model homes and identify imaginative and creative designs that involve a minimum of expense. Determine how this was done. Also be aware of ideas that were not quite successful in their implementation.

- Plan how you might revitalize a piece of furniture or accessory in your home. Take into consideration other furnishings that will be used with it.

## Optional Readings

*Better Homes and Gardens Decorating Ideas under $100.* Des Moines: Better Homes and Gardens, 1971. A book filled with a multitude of ideas that are unique and individual.

*Good Housekeeping Decorating and Do-It-Yourself.* London: The Hearst Corporation, 1977. Provides practical as well as economical solutions. Deals with overall plan and specific areas. Includes many money-saving projects.

Stepat-DeVan, Dorothy. *Introduction to Home Furnishings.* New York: The Macmillan Co., 1971. Pages 249–53. General coverage of stretching the dollar when purchasing home furnishings.

Wallach, Carla. *Interior Decorating with Plants.* New York: The Macmillan Co., 1976. Pages 47–48. Specific minimum budget ideas. Entire book offers many good ideas.

# WHERE TO GO FROM HERE

**30**

## FROM HERE

A Final Note

**Assignments for Unit Thirty**

1. Read the Overview, Student Learning Objectives, and Learning Supplement for this unit.

2. Watch Television Program Thirty, "Where to Go from Here."

3. Consider Key Terms and Concepts.

4. Complete the Learning Activities.

5. Review the Student Learning Objectives.

## Overview

Men and women of all ages, whether they live alone or in family units, enjoy shaping their interior environment. As you approach this lesson, you will have a good foundation upon which to base decisions related to planning interiors and selecting furnishings. Although this telecourse represents a basic, comprehensive coverage of the many facets of interior planning, it does not provide solutions for every unique design problem. But you should continue to grow in confidence and in your ability to use techniques of design. Stay abreast of technological advances in interior products and make use of the many excellent educational resources available.

Publications such as magazines, newspaper supplements, and manufacturers' brochures provide easy and inexpensive ways to acquire additional design and product information. Local stores that specialize in home furnishings frequently offer educational seminars and "miniclasses." Keep in mind that even though you continue to study, you may be receiving only one person's point of view. Therefore, it is important that you evaluate material objectively and always consider your personal viewpoint as a valid one.

If you desire to develop a more comprehensive design background for your own use, investigate the opportunities provided by your local educational institutions and governmental agencies. For example, parks and recreation departments, state agricultural extension offices, community colleges, and adult educational programs offer classes in the subjects of color theory, history of art, woodworking, and upholstery. These classes can provide excellent supplemental information. In addition to spending time and effort, you may also have to pay an enrollment fee, so it is wise to evaluate these programs to determine their value to you.

Even with a good background in interior design you may need occasional help from a trained professional. Perhaps you need approval of your ideas, or require consultation on a difficult design problem. Maybe you have determined that you have insufficient time to devote to your project and could really use some additional help. At times such as these the services of a professional interior designer are invaluable.

A suitable designer can save you time by bringing new products to your attention, offering unique solutions to problems, and providing access to all resources such as craftsmen, manufacturers, and suppliers. In addition, the professional can handle many of the details necessary in the ordering, delivery, and installation of required merchandise. The designer's experience and education can help prevent errors, which in turn, can offset the cost of his or her services. The interior design knowledge that you have acquired will aid in communication.

There are different types of professional design assistance available at varied costs. Some designers will contract only full-concept assignments; others accept smaller jobs, such as providing background suggestions, designs for single rooms, or simply consultation. Some stores maintain a staff of designers for their customers. These designers will create, at no cost to the customer, interior plans that utilize merchandise found in that particular store. If a customer is satisfied with the designer's plans and ideas, an unwritten consumer responsibility is to purchase the products from this professional and his store. In other words, do not pick a designer's brains for free and then purchase elsewhere.

Friends' homes, furnished model homes, store displays, and rooms featured in publications all represent opportunities for you to evaluate a designer's completed product before choosing one individual. References from the local or national headquarters of the American Society of Interior Designers are available at your request. Additional sources of designers are telephone directories and advertisements. If you are not familiar with a particular designer, it is always good practice to request to see some examples of his or her work.

Other criteria to consider when you select a professional designer include personal qualities, professional preparation, professional ethics, and cost. To know and evaluate these, both parties must be able to establish open and honest communications.

Whether you choose to work with an independent interior designer, an affiliate of a design corporation, or perhaps a store-based designer, it is important to understand and evaluate the type of payment required for the services rendered. Here are some of the more common methods used by designers for compensation:

- Flat fee: one charge for merchandise and designer's services

- Flat fee plus percentage: designer's fee plus percentage of all costs over the original budget

- Hourly and per diem fee: used usually for consultations, shopping time, problem-solving, etc.

- Merchandise at retail: designer charges client for merchandise at list price

- Cost plus percentage: fee figured by adding an agreed percentage to the cost of materials

Although many states do not, as yet, require licensing of interior designers, responsible professionals usually begin their careers with a sound educational background and continue to update and broaden their knowledge. Not all good interior designers choose to belong to the professional organization, the American Society of Interior Designers (ASID). However, membership indicates that the individual meets rigid educational standards, possesses considerable experience, and adheres to a professional code of ethics.

## Student Learning Objectives

When you complete Unit Thirty, you should be able to do the following:

- Explain the importance of continuing to learn and keeping up-to-date in the field of interior design and suggest at least three methods the consumer may follow to accomplish this goal.

- Determine the need for and the value of a professional interior designer in relation to your own design projects. Suggest criteria you would use when selecting an interior designer.

- Discuss the responsibilities between an interior designer and a consumer that are necessary to establish a satisfactory working relationship.

## Learning Supplement

This one course alone cannot prepare you for a career in interior design. However, if you are interested in this field, an overall assessment of your personal qualities, employment opportunities, and educational requirements would be most beneficial. Keep in mind, too, there are a number of related careers that require different amounts and types of education and abilities. Careers such as showroom employee, perspective and sketch artist, drafter, and display designer represent opportunities to use your interior-design talent and education.

Whether you are selecting a professional interior designer or considering interior design as a career, there are certain personal and professional qualities recognized as desirable. Because the profession is strongly people-oriented, an understanding of human behavior and an ability to communicate and work with all types of individuals is essential. Also, a sensitivity to the feelings, ideas, and unique needs of clients is required. Besides the ability to design interiors and work with people, success in this profession usually follows only if the individual applies organized thinking, problem-solving techniques, systematic work habits, and good, ethical business practices.

Competition in the field of interior design and its allied industries is intense. Although there are indications that the job market for designers will continue to grow, interested students should make a thorough assessment of the future opportunities in their own geographical locations. It may be necessary for the qualified person to enter this field through a related position or as an apprentice.

## Key Terms and Concepts
Related careers
ASID

Flat fee

Flat fee plus percentage

Merchandise at retail

Cost plus percentage

## Learning Activities

- What are six personal or professional qualities considered essential in a professional interior designer? Discuss how a lack of one or more of these qualities could affect a client/professional working relationship.

- Explain the benefit to the consumer of obtaining some knowledge in interior design.

- Identify four available resources to use to add to or update your interior design knowledge. How should you assess the resources in relation to your needs?

- Analyze how to select an interior designer to best satisfy your needs.

- Determine the value of using professional design services for your own situation.

- Identify four problems that could result when a client and professional designer do not establish a good working relationship. Suggest steps that could have been followed to prevent these problems.

## Optional Activities

If a career in interior design seems appealing to you, you may wish to complete one or more of the following activities:

- Interview a professional designer. Try to determine such things as job satisfaction, work pressures, and salary.

- Assess the future interior-design job market in your area. Determine opportunities for entering this profession through related fields.

- Evaluate the interior-design programs of the public and private educational institutions in your location. Try to determine cost, placement of graduates, and quality of program.

- Request career brochures from the American Society of Interior Designers, 730 Fifth Avenue, New York, New York 10019. Suggested brochures are: "Membership Information," "Interior Design Career Guide," "Fact Sheet," and "Code of Ethics."

## Optional Reading

Sulahria, Julie, and Diamond, Ruby. *Inside Design: Creating Your Environment.* San Francisco: Canfield Press, 1977. "Epilogue—Interior Design Careers." Pages 303-11. Good study of career goals. Updated career information.